D0467212

THE CENTERS OF CIVILIZATION SERIES

(*Complete list on page* 165)

KYOTO
in the Momoyama Period

BY WENDELL COLE

UNIVERSITY OF OKLAHOMA PRESS : NORMAN

The paper on which this book is printed bears the watermark of the University of Oklahoma Press and is designed for an effective life of at least three hundred years.

Library of Congress Catalog Card Number: 67–15586

 Composed and printed at Norman, Oklahoma, U.S.A., by the University of Oklahoma Press. First edition.

To Charlotte

Preface

THE NAME KYOTO, composed of two Chinese ideograms meaning "capital" and "metropolis," has been used only since 1870 to designate the city which was the imperial capital of Japan for more than a thousand years. In 1869 the imperial court was moved to Edo, which was renamed Tokyo (Eastern Capital), and an unsuccessful attempt was made to refer to the former imperial capital as Saikyo (Western Capital). At the time Kyoto was founded in 794, its official name was Heian-kyo, or Capital of Peace and Tranquillity. In succeeding centuries the Japanese people most commonly knew it simply as the "Capital," Kyo or Miyako, and when the Jesuit priests and Portuguese traders arrived toward the middle of the sixteenth century, it was by the latter name that they first learned of the city. The European travelers who later wrote reports used the spelling Meaco, which seemed to be as close as they could come to what the Japanese called it.

Still another term is found in Japanese literary references to Kyoto. During the Heian Period the left or east side of the city experienced the greatest growth and was known as Raku or Rakuyo. Originally Rakuyo seems to have been derived from Lo-Yang, the Chinese T'ang Dynasty capital which had impressed Japanese scholars and diplomats as a cosmopolitan center of Chinese culture. At first Rakuyo was applied only to Sakyo, or the left capital area, but it was afterward extended to indicate the whole city, particularly in poetry and other literary works. During the Momoyama Period it was especially fashionable for writers to use Raku or Rakuyo when mentioning the capital. Most of the citizens, however, customarily referred to their city as Miyako.

Momoyama is a name employed by Japanese writers in recent times for the period when the three great sixteenth century military rulers, Oda Nobunaga, Toyotomi Hideyoshi, and Tokugawa Ieyasu, were achieving the unification of Japan. From 1568 when the troops of Nobunaga occupied Kyoto until the first decade of the seventeenth century when Ieyasu chose Edo (modern Tokyo) as the administrative capital of Japan, Kyoto was the focal point of political, social, economic, and artistic forces which brought about a new and splendid age. The Japanese term Momoyama Jidai, "Peach Hill Period," was not used in the sixteenth century but originated from the fact that in 1594 Hideyoshi built himself a castle on a hill at Fushimi, near the southern edge of Kyoto, from which he planned to supervise the administration of the Japanese Empire. After Hideyoshi's death in 1598, this castle was dismantled, and about a hundred years later the whole hillside on which the castle had stood was planted with peach trees; hence the popular designation of the age of Hideyoshi as the Peach Hill Period. The first three-quarters of the sixteenth century until the flight of the deposed Ashikaga shogun in 1573 is usually considered part of the Muromachi Period, named for the street in Kyoto where the Ashikaga palace had been built.

Because of the vast political, social, and artistic changes which occurred, the Momoyama Period has been described as a time in which every decade was equal to a century in other ages. Although it lasted only about forty years, it is one of the most significant in the entire history of Japan, for it was during this era that the foundations of modern Japan were established. When it began, the country was just emerging from centuries of anarchy, bloodshed, and destruction; when it ended four decades later, Tokugawa Ieyasu had made himself the absolute ruler of a united nation, and Japan was entering a period of 250 years of isolation, peace, and quiescence.

I wish especially to thank Arthur Voyce, who encouraged me to write this book; the Stanford University School of Humanities and Sciences, which granted me the necessary time; and the Graduate Division of the University which provided assistance in typing the manuscript.

WENDELL COLE

Stanford, California
March 8, 1967

Contents

	Preface	ix
1.	Miyako, the Capital City	3
2.	The Three Heroes	27
3.	Rakuchu, or Within the Capital	54
4.	Shinto, Buddhism, and Kiristitan	88
5.	Matsu, Kabuki, and Other Pleasures	104
6.	The Great Decorators	123
7.	Epilogue	144
	Selected Bibliography	149
	Index	153
	May of Kyoto	5

KYOTO
in the Momoyama Period

1

Miyako, the Capital City

ON A CHILL, GRAY DAY toward the middle of January, 1551, Francis Xavier, the "Apostle of the East," reached Kyoto for the first time. Before him as he approached the city from the south lay a desolate, uncultivated plain, stretching for miles and scattered with burned and ruined buildings. Among the dark and forbidding pine forests on the slopes of the snow-covered mountains which surrounded the city on three sides was the charred wreckage of temples and shrines. Along the ravaged streets, attempts had been made to patch together old boards and strips of bark to provide refuge from the icy winds sweeping down from the mountains, and only an occasional building of one or two stories with clay-covered walls and gray shingled roofs seemed to offer a measure of shelter from the marrow-chilling cold. Many of the men who crowded through the city gates straining at great carts or bent over with huge loads on their backs wore nothing but a short ragged cloak, and their legs and arms were bare despite the bitter weather. Everywhere were throngs of wretched beggars, some of them tiny children, and incoming travelers were pursued by pitiful young girls soliciting for the disreputable inns that huddled together along the road. This magnificent capital city's haunting beauty and elegant society had been praised by Japanese poets and delineated by Japanese painters for more than 750 years. Xavier was understandably disappointed and discouraged.

He had been in Japan since August, 1549, when he had landed at Kagoshima in southwestern Kyushu. There with the permission of the daimyo, or lord of the province of Satsuma, he and his two Jesuit companions had begun to preach and attempt conversions. These three missionaries were not the first Europeans to arrive in Japan, for sometime in 1542, or possibly as late as the autumn of 1543, three Portuguese who had taken passage in a Chinese junk for Macao were driven north by a typhoon and landed on Tanegashima, a small island twenty-five miles off the southern coast of Kyushu. Before Xavier's arrival in 1549, several Portuguese merchant ships had called at harbors in Kyushu, and between 1543 and 1549, Portuguese traders had reached as far as Kyoto on the main island of Honshu.

After a year of missionary activity in western Japan, Xavier was eager to visit Kyoto, for the capital had been reported by the Portuguese merchants to be a vast city with an estimated population of 500,000. By October, 1550, Xavier had made up his mind to travel to Kyoto and seek permission from the Emperor to carry on his work of conversion in the capital itself. With a lay brother of the Society of Jesus, Juan Fernandez, who had formerly been a wealthy silk merchant in Portugal, Xavier set out for Kyoto. The appearance of the foreigners was so odd-looking and their clothing so shabby that no one would give them shelter. Xavier, who was dressed in a ragged cotton cassock and with his feet bare, suffered greatly from the wind, rain, and snow. As they wandered from town to town along the Inland Sea, they were jeered at and stoned by mocking children and attacked by snarling dogs. At last they arrived at the thriving port of Sakai near the mouth of the Yodo

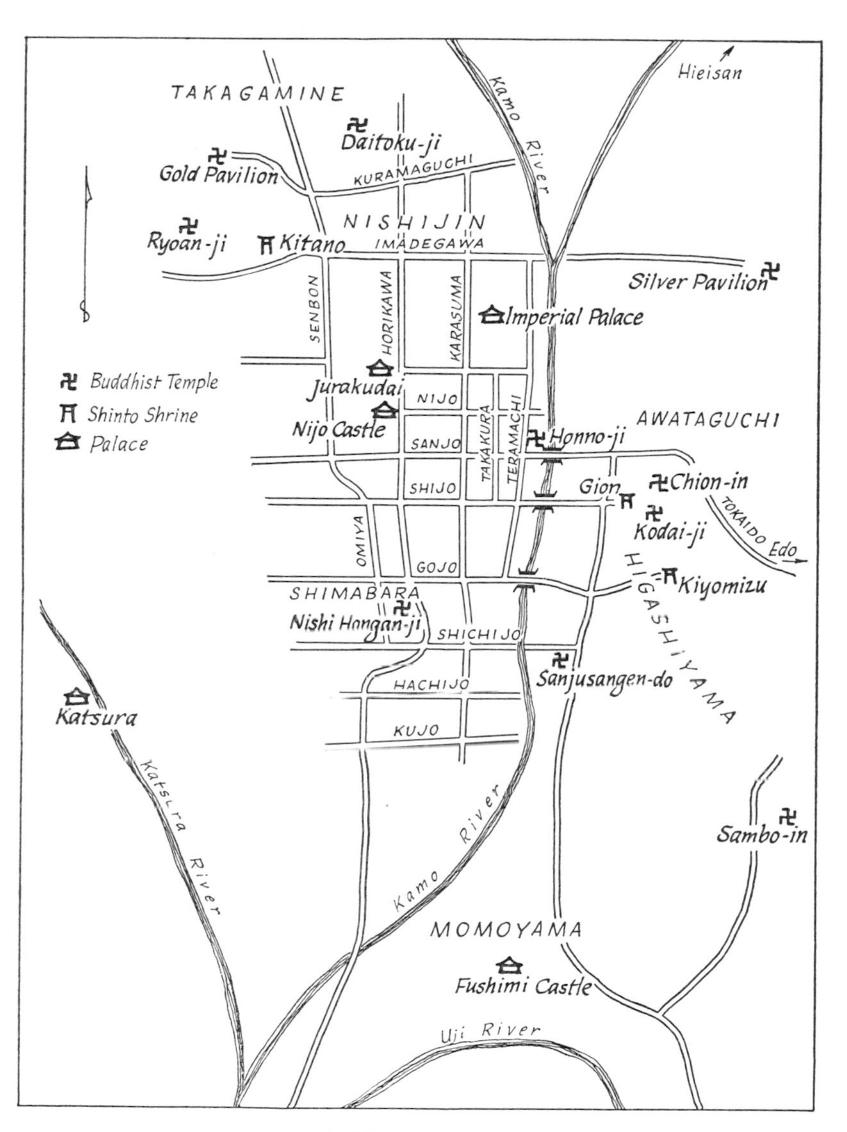
TAKAGAMINE
Daitoku-ji
Gold Pavilion
KURAMAGUCHI
Kamo River
Hieisan
NISHIJIN
Ryoan-ji
Kitano
IMADEGAWA
Silver Pavilion
SENBON
HORIKAWA
KARASUMA
Imperial Palace
Buddhist Temple
Shinto Shrine
Palace
Jurakudai
NIJO
Nijo Castle
TAKAKURA
TERAMACHI
AWATAGUCHI
Honno-ji
SANJO
SHIJO
Gion
Chion-in
Kodai-ji
TOKAIDO
Edo
OMIYA
GOJO
HIGASHIYAMA
Kiyomizu
SHIMABARA
Nishi Hongan-ji
SHICHIJO
Sanjusangen-do
HACHIJO
Katsura
KUJO
Katsura River
Kamo River
Sambo-in
MOMOYAMA
Fushimi Castle
Uji River

MAP OF KYOTO

River on Osaka Bay. There they learned that the area surrounding Kyoto had been in a state of war for many years and that anyone who persisted in living in the city ran the risk of being slaughtered, burned, or starved. Xavier was determined to continue, and through an introduction to a Japanese gentleman who was traveling to the capital, the two Jesuits were allowed to join his servants for the trip along the Yodo up to Kyoto. In spite of ominous warnings, Xavier and Fernandez must have been ill prepared for such a scene of utter destruction as they found in the capital.

"This city of Miyako had been very important," wrote Xavier in a letter from Cochin, January 29, 1552: "Today because of wars, it is in most part destroyed; many of the people told us that formerly it had 18,000 houses, and it seemed to me that this was indeed the truth according to its very large site. Now, in fact, it is destroyed and burned."

The first foreigners in Japan had little understanding of the Japanese political system, which was then in a state of complete anarchy, but Xavier hoped to obtain an authorization to preach in Kyoto from the ruling monarch. When he arrived in January, 1551, however, the Shogun Yoshiteru, who was nominally the military ruler of the country, had been hunted from the capital by his own first minister, Miyoshi; and the emperor, Go Nara, was living in poverty and obscurity. Xavier did not know that to visit the emperor was a privilege granted to very few, and that an audience was quite beyond the reach of a foreigner whose strange appearance and poor clothes made him an object of ridicule. Realizing that he could accomplish nothing amid the lawless and disorganized city, Xavier left Kyoto after a stay of only eleven days. He had, nevertheless, made several discoveries which were to be important in the future to the Portuguese missionaries and traders. Neither the emperor nor the shogun, he had found, had any real power, for the central government in Kyoto had collapsed completely. When Xavier stepped into the boat which was to convey him down the Yodo to Osaka Bay, perhaps he did not realize it, but he was leaving Kyoto never to return.

At the time of Xavier's visit in 1551, Kyoto had been the capital of Japan and the residence of the emperor for 756 years, with the exception of one short interval of scarcely six months in 1180 when Taira-no-Kiyomori, the military dictator, had taken the imperial court to Fukuhara near Kobe. During one other period, from 1192 to 1333, the real seat of the military administration, or Bakufu, had been moved to Kamakura in eastern Japan. When the Ashikaga family came into power in the fourteenth century, the shogunate had been returned to Kyoto.

In the early history of Japan it had been customary to move the capital to a new location upon the death of the emperor, for the belief was held at that time that the passing of a divine ruler defiled the area in which he died. From 710 to 782, however, a permanent capital had been established at Nara, about twenty-six miles south of Kyoto. In 782 the Emperor Kammu decided to move from Nara, apparently to escape from the increasing political interference of the Buddhist monks in the old capital. Work had progressed on a new site at Nagaoka for a decade when suddenly Kammu decided to move again. His decision was perhaps determined by various deaths and family misfortunes which were imputed to an unfavorable location. With the aid of diviners and geomancers another site was selected about five miles northeast of Nagaoka. After announcements were made to the sun goddess, to the tutelary deities of the locality, and to the Emperor's ancestors, work was commenced in 793 on the new capital.

The site selected for Kyoto, near the Yodo River which was navigable to Osaka Bay, was a flat plain gently sloping toward the south and dotted with pine and bamboo groves. The eastern boundary was formed by the Kamo River, the western by the Katsura. The water of these rivers was noted for its unusual clarity, and even if it was not responsible, as legend reported, for the beauty of those Kyoto maidens dipped in it at birth, it was to prove extremely important to the success of the Kyoto cloth dyeing industry in later centuries. On all sides except the south were uninhabited mountains densely grown with pines and cypresses. Not close enough to cast their shadows on the city, these mountains presented a background of exceptional loveliness. Across the Kamo to the east was Higashiyama (Eastern Hills), and to the northeast was 2,600-foot Hieisan (Wisdom Mountain). The latter was of particular significance since the northeast, a traditionally malignant direction according to the Chinese cosmological scheme, was called in Japanese *kimon*, the devil's gate.

In 788 the monk Saicho had propitiously established a temple, the Enryaku-ji, on Hieisan which, it was hoped, would protect the new city from the evil spirits of the northeast quarter. As it turned out, it was the monks of the Enryaku-ji from whom the city needed protection. Five miles to the east on the other side of Higashiyama and Hieisan was Biwa-ko, the largest lake in Japan.

To the south was the Gokinai (Five Province) plain, an abundantly fertile region of alluvial soil covering about five hundred square miles at the head of Osaka Bay. The weather of the Gokinai was unusually variable with rain, wind, and overhanging clouds. The summer monsoons from the south brought a heavy rainfall which created a climate that was almost subtropical. In the winter the winds blew from the north, and snow frequently crowned the bordering mountains. Throughout much of the year the mists and fog enveloped the mountains and the city in a lovely shimmering haze which was to inspire countless painters and poets. The new city was soon surrounded by a mosaic of diked fields where rice was sown in the May rains. In summer these fields disappeared under the vivid green of young rice; in September they were golden with the harvest, and in winter empty and brown and spiked with conical straw ricks. Because the rains, which often reached flood proportions, carried away soluble materials from the soil, the farmers were obliged to use great quantities of fertilizer, but the climate also made it possible to raise an additional crop of other grains or vegetables in the same fields each year.

Like Nara, the new capital of Heian-kyo was laid out symmetrically on the plan of the Chinese Sui Dynasty capital at Ch'ang-an. Not only the grand scale of the city plan but the architecture, court costumes, etiquette, bureaucracy, written language, and literature were all borrowed from China. A broad highway 250 feet wide named the Shujaku split the city into two halves called the East and West or Left (Sakyo) Capital and Right (Ukyo) Capital. At the northern end of this avenue stood the Daidairi, or Great Palace Enclosure. The entrance to the Shujaku from the south was through an immense seven-portaled gate, the Rashomon. The rest of the city was marked off like a huge checkerboard by the roads which traversed it at regular intervals from north to south and east to west. Parallel to the Shujaku ran eight avenues 80 to 120 feet wide, called *oji;*

at right angles were nine east-west avenues, the *jo*, which were known by numbers from Ichijo, First Avenue, to Kujo, Ninth Avenue. The Daidairi lay between Ichijo and the 170-foot-wide Nijo (Second Avenue). Four-hundred-foot square areas called *cho* enclosed by the principal roads were divided into thirty-two residential lots of fifty feet by one hundred feet.

The whole city was surrounded by an embankment and ditch and was intersected from north to south by six canalized streams. Measured from north to south the capital covered nearly three and one-half miles, and about two and one-half miles from east to west. Construction began in 793, and the Emperor was able to move into his new palace in 795, even though some of the buildings in the Daidairi were not completed until 806. The imperial residence was called the Kokyo, an assemblage of some thirty pavilions making up a palace of unparalleled splendor.

Although the period from the ninth to the twelfth century was one of almost four hundred years of unbroken peace during which the imperial court made Kyoto the center of Japanese culture and refinement, the original planning of the city proved too grand. The western half, or Right Capital, was never fully developed, possibly because it was low and damp. It began to decline within fifty years until, by the end of the Heian Period in the twelfth century, it was almost deserted except for scattered mansions falling into disrepair and some houses along a few streets adjacent to the Daidairi. The tendency was to expand to the north and east. By 1200, many of the main streets running from west to east had been continued across the Kamo River, extending the city as far as Higashiyama. Among a series of five or six new streets laid out north of the Great Palace Enclosure, the most important was Imadegawa. The lack of good building stone, and a wealth of forests had influenced the Japanese to create a wooden architecture which suffered extensive damage from earthquakes, *Tai-fu* ("great winds"), and fires which by the twelfth century had destroyed most of the original Heian city. Conflagrations in 1177 and 1188 swept through many public buildings and thousands of dwellings. The palace, already badly damaged, became uninhabitable after a fire in 1228, and the Great Palace Enclosure fell gradually into disuse. For the next 350 years the emperors lived in various temporary or detached palaces. These were generally in the northern part of the city between Ichijo and Nijo. Probably by 1228 not a single building remained in Kyoto from the early Heian city. After the Ashikaga shoguns moved the Bakufu back to Kyoto in the fourteenth century, the capital was almost entirely rebuilt.

The political system of the shogunate had evolved in the twelfth century when Minamoto Yoritomo (1147–99) defeated his military rivals, the Taira family, had himself appointed (1192) the Sei-tai-Shogun (Barbarian-Subduing Generalissimo) by the envoys of the emperor, and founded at Kamakura in eastern Japan a military dictatorship. On earlier occasions the title of shogun ("army leader") had been granted to generals appointed by the emperor to quell revolts against the imperial government. When they had accomplished this purpose, the title was revoked, but in 1192 the Shogun, entrusted with the entire administration of the empire, instituted a permanent system called the Bakufu or Camp Capital.

The Kamakura government was staffed by warriors of the *buke* class, the samurai and daimyo. The samurai ("one who serves") were vassals who owed allegiance to a lord or daimyo ("great name"). Because Minamoto Yoritomo had received from the Emperor a perpetual commission as chief of the military governors and tax administrators, in the future no one but a member of the Minamoto family could ever become shogun. As a consequence, the first two of the three military rulers who brought about the unification of Japan in the sixteenth century were never able to assume the title of shogun since they could not prove descent from the Minamotos.

For more than two hundred years the shogun ruled in Kamakura in a stern samurai tradition, while in Kyoto the emperor and the court nobles intrigued to overthrow him. This dual system continued until the Kamakura government was challenged in 1333 by the Emperor Go Daigo, supported by members of the Kyoto nobility and various dissatisfied samurai. Go Daigo was unable to obtain control, and two separate courts struggled for the imperial throne. By 1336 a new shogunate had been set up in Kyoto by Ashikaga Takauji (1305–58).

Conflicts continued for almost sixty years until Ashikaga Yoshimitsu (1358–1408), the grandson of Takauji, consolidated his power as shogun (1392). Yoshimitsu was not just a clever politician. Increasingly attracted by the pattern of aristocratic life in Kyoto, he took every means to temper the rough and warlike spirit of the samurai by urging his officials to adopt the polished manners and refined tastes of the court nobles. Buddhism encouraged early retirement, and Yoshimitsu was only too willing to spend his time building the famous Gold Pavilion (1397), writing poetry, commissioning paintings, collecting lacquer and pottery, and giving lavish parties. About the only religious aspects of his retirement were Buddhist touches in the architecture of the Gold Pavilion and in his monastic dress.

The shoguns who followed Yoshimitsu were unable to

maintain authority over the empire, and by the time Ashikaga Yoshimasa (1435–90) became shogun, the government was so weakened it controlled only the city of Kyoto and its environs. The rest of the country had fallen into complete anarchy with each daimyo attempting to seize as many neighboring fiefs as he could obtain by treachery or force. Yoshimasa was actually a puppet under the domination of the *Kanrei*, the shogun's deputy. In 1464 Yoshimasa, then only thirty, decided to retire since his duties as shogun interfered with his pleasures. By 1467 the Hosokawa and Yamana families, who supplied the leading candidates for the post of *Kanrei*, became involved in an argument between Yoshimasa and his brother Yoshimi over the appointment of Yoshimasa's successor as shogun. When Yoshimasa was supported by Yamana, Yoshimi's cause was taken up by Yamana's son-in-law, Hosokawa Katsumoto. Yamana camped in southwestern Kyoto with a force of 90,000, and Hosokawa occupied northeastern Kyoto with an army of 100,000. In the decade of conflict which followed, known as the Onin War, Kyoto was so completely devastated that a century was to pass before it was finally rebuilt.

While the retired Yoshimasa looked for an attractive site on which to erect his Ginkaku (Silver Pavilion), the imperial palace, the mansions of the nobility, and the homes of the citizens were all laid waste. At the close of 1467 a Bakufu official described the capital as "an empty field from which the evening skylark rises with songs and descends among tears." As the delicate gray and white Ginkaku was being constructed in a garden on Higashiyama, the people of Kyoto were starving, and the streets were piled with skeletons. Yoshimasa's government was exceptionally bad, for it was both ruinously extravagant and unbelievably corrupt, but Ashikaga-Muromachi culture reached its height under him. He lavishly supported playwrights, actors, dancers, musicians, artists, and architects. The tea ceremony was raised to a fine art, he patronized magnificent productions of No plays, and the architect and garden designer, Soami, created for him the renowned Ginkaku. Yoshimasa's death in 1490 brought to a close the greatest days of Muromachi culture.

The Onin War had ended in the Kyoto area in 1477, but the conflict spread to the provinces and by 1500 almost the whole of Japan was at war. The century which followed is aptly known to Japanese historians as Sengoku Jidai, the Age of the Country at War. When the rival armies had finally been withdrawn from Kyoto in 1477, the city presented a picture of almost complete destruction. During the two months of January and February, 1480, as many as 82,000 people died of starvation and disease in the capital. The city was cut off from communications in all directions by the plundering armies, and incoming rice was held up at toll barriers where exorbitant taxes were demanded by collectors in the employ of the war lords. Some accounts estimate that by the close of the century the population of the city had been reduced from half a million to fewer than 40,000 residents. For a time after the war the capital was in the hands of lawless marauders who camped at the To-ji temple and Gion shrine and robbed and murdered the citizens. The people were so demoralized, according to one chronicle, that robbery and gambling were the chief occupations.

If a strong shogun had been able to enforce peace, the capital would have had an opportunity to recover from the Onin War, but as the sixteenth century advanced, the shogunate became even weaker than before. By 1550 the shoguns had far less wealth and security than the daimyo in the provinces. In actual practice, Kyoto itself was governed by the *Kanrei*, the shogun's deputy, who held the only real power. The fate of Yoshiteru, who was shogun when Xavier arrived in Kyoto in 1551, is indicative of the wretched condition of the shoguns. He had assumed the office in 1545 upon the retirement of his father Yoshiharu. The administration was in complete chaos, the courts were filled with undecided cases, the oppressive taxes were impossible to collect, and the government was unable to pay its officials or even to supply them with food. The guards deserted the shogun's mansion, and during Xavier's visit to Kyoto, Yoshiteru was in hiding from his own deputy, the *Kanrei*.

In an incredibly bizarre situation, the political struggles by that time were not between claimants to the offices of emperor or shogun, but to the more powerful office of *Kanrei*. In 1558 a treacherous Hosokawa vassal named Miyoshi and his retainer Matsunaga defeated the last of the Hosokawa deputies. Fourteen years after Xavier's visit, Matsunaga, by then the chief minister of the shogunate, attacked the shogun's mansion, which was being rebuilt, and Yoshiteru was murdered. Three years after his death, Nobunaga, the first of the great military rulers of the sixteenth century, entered Kyoto as its conqueror.

By the sixteenth century more than two hundred years had passed since the emperor had attempted to exert any political authority, yet the throne was still an object of veneration. As the emperor himself usually had several wives and many children, there were constant quarrels over the royal succession, complicated by the custom of abdication at an early age. Like the later Ashikaga shoguns, the emperors were anxious to escape from wearisome court ceremonies to a mansion in the hills from which they could continue court intrigues while presumably living in holy seclusion. In spite of the turmoil which often surrounded accession to the throne, the claims of divine ancestry and of unbroken succession were never abandoned. All too frequently the reigning emperor was a very young child at the mercy of regents or other court officials.

While the court had lost every vestige of its political powers, its ranks and titles were still bestowed by the emperor, and members of the *buke*, or warrior class, were absurdly eager to receive these empty honors. Nevertheless, it was upon the *kuge*, or court nobles, that they were conferred, and the poorest *kuge* by far outranked a daimyo who was the ruler of several provinces. Just as medieval European kings never considered abolishing the office of the pope, no matter how badly they might treat the incumbent, to the shogun and the daimyo the emperor was more like the deity than his representative.

Until the end of the fifteenth century the shoguns and emperors had been on cordial terms and often entertained each other elaborately, as long as they had any money to do so. When the Tsuchi-mikado Palace was burned (1477), the Emperor fled to the Shogun's mansion, and most of the court nobles sought refuge with daimyo outside the Gokinai area. In 1478, attempts were made to rebuild the palace, but the Emperor had no funds and was dependent on contributions from loyal daimyo just to keep alive. Since there were no buildings in which to hold them, the great court festivals could no longer be observed, and even the Senyo-den, the depository for the sacred mirror which had enticed from her cave the sun goddess-ancestress of the Japanese nation, was in ruins. Under Yoshimitsu a handsome income from neighboring rice lands had been provided for the Emperor and his court, but the constant warfare in Kyoto and its vicinity after 1467 had made almost all agriculture impossible. The domains charged with the support of the imperial house returned no revenue whatsoever. Although some reports may be tales fabricated for political purposes, sixteenth century records are filled with accounts of the poverty of the Emperor and the nobility. In reality, it is probable that the Emperor was very short of funds but not completely destitute.

In 1500 when Emperor Go Tsuchi-mikado (1465–1500) died on the throne, having been too poor even to retire, his body was not buried for six weeks until money could be found for his funeral expenses. His successor, Go Kashiwabara (1500–28), reigned for more than twenty years before the Hongan-ji monks collected enough to pay for his enthronement ceremonies. When Go Kashiwabara died in 1528, the Shogun arranged for his funeral but did not provide for the accession of the next emperor, Go Nara (1528–58), who had to wait ten years to be enthroned. The fortunes of the throne probably reached their nadir in the reign of Go Nara, emperor when Xavier arrived in Kyoto in 1551. A contemporary Japanese record, *Rojin Zatsuwa*, pictures the palace as hardly distinguishable from a peasant's hut. The Emperor was reduced to selling his autograph as well as precious household utensils. It was reported that any citizen of Kyoto with a few coins or a bowl of rice might leave a request at the Emperor's gate asking him to copy a certain verse from the *Hundred Poets' Songs*, and in a few days the example of the Emperor's calligraphy would appear. Although the emperor had not made a public appearance for more than a century, it was said that there were many times after 1500 when anyone who wished could stare through the broken bamboo fence around the palace and see members of the imperial household at their daily tasks.

Leading nobles, who despised the warrior class, earned a precarious living by teaching court etiquette, music, and art appreciation to those samurai who had social ambitions. One account declares that in 1568 when the troops of Nobunaga occupied Kyoto, Emperor Ogimachi (1558–87) held a banquet at which the only food was noodle soup. The court nobles, rumored to be subsisting on rice cakes and soup made from stray dogs, with wild ducks which could be caught in the rice fields an infrequent delicacy, were described as pathetically thankful for a gift of dried persimmons or a few bean cakes.

It was not the shogun or the aristocracy who began the reconstruction of Kyoto but the merchants and craftsmen who returned after the wars. Most of these men were artisans producing goods for sale in the city; others were merchants importing commodities from outside Kyoto. Reconstruction was carried on under the leadership of the *za*, the guilds or corporations into which the merchants and artisans of Kyoto had been organized since the fourteenth century. *Za* means "seat" and originally indicated the attachment of the guild to a shrine or temple. Late in the sixteenth century *za* came to be used as the word for "theater" since the first companies of musicians, dancers, and actors were attached to shrines. The Kyoto *za* included such diverse groups as woodworkers, brewers, soy cookers, paper hangers, potters, painters, copperworkers, umbrella makers, and architects. Great quantities of raw silk had been imported from China in the fifteenth century, and one of the largest *za* was composed of the weavers who had been uncommonly prosperous before the Onin War forced them to abandon their looms. Merchants and artisans who were not *za-shu* (guild members) could transact only a very limited amount of business. All of the members of a typical *za* were grouped in one street or area, and no one not in that *za* was allowed to conduct business there.

In spite of plundering daimyo and Ashikaga tax collectors, the *za* of the sake merchants, the warehouse keepers, and the bean-cake sellers had all been successful in accumulating capital and in the fifteenth century were the principal moneylenders. For a hundred years after the Onin Era these moneylenders were the unwilling victims of riots by the lower classes who demanded release from their debts. The Ashikaga shoguns began the practice of quieting the rioters by issuing the *tokusei* ("benevolent administration") which released the debtor completely on payment of ten per cent of the original debt. The *tokusei* was misused by the shoguns to such an extent that contemporary commentators felt that it was contributing to the moral disintegration of the time. If debts could be canceled by this easy method, frugality was foolish and saving useless.

In the fifteenth century the daimyo had discovered that they could increase their revenues by erecting toll barriers across the roads; about 1450 there were over six hundred toll stations in a distance of thirty miles between Kyoto and Osaka Bay along the Yodo River. These taxes together with the numerous highwaymen caused a decrease in the amount of goods sent into Kyoto after the war and prevented the passage of food to such an extent that the capital suffered a series of terrible famines. Kyoto was no longer the principal center of trade and industry in Japan, as it had been, but only one of several towns which were commercial centers for their surrounding regions. The Kyoto citizens were further harassed when the shogunate levied a house tax to make up for the declining income from the shogun's estates.

Commerce and industry grew after 1500 despite the unsettled conditions of the early century, and the fires, riots, and high taxes did not prevent the merchants and artisans from rebuilding many streets in the capital. Before long Sanjo and Shijo were once more lined with shops, and travelers and traders were beginning to appear in increasing numbers. The *za* set up autonomous organizations called *machigumi*, or block committees, to govern and defend themselves, since the power of the Emperor or Shogun to protect them had completely disintegrated. The leaders in the *machigumi* were the prosperous sake merchants and other moneylenders who became virtual governors of the city through their control of wealth. In the provinces the daimyo ruled their own vassals, organized their own armies, and enforced their own laws. Previous to the Onin War there were about 260 feudal houses, but by 1600 all but a dozen or so had disappeared, leaving the way clear for the rise of an entirely new warrior class. The first half of the century, in particular, was a time when the weaker daimyo were eliminated in a violent rearrangement of social classes.

As the ancient feudal families succumbed, many leaderless samurai called *ronin*, or "wave men," drifted to Kyoto or took service away from their home areas. The necessity for raising large armies forced the daimyo to make use of serfs and peasants as soldiers. These conscripts, formerly farmers forbidden to leave their farms, were known as *ashigaru* (foot soldiers). One effect of this demand for soldiers was to break up the "serfdom of a thousand years," for many never returned to their farms. Leaderless samurai and landless serfs poured into Kyoto as the countryside was overrun by armies. These displaced men, from widely disparate social classes, had no means of supporting themselves in the city and turned to insurrection with demands for food and government assistance. The leaders of these riots were often caught and executed by the Bakufu, but the shogunate was incapable of preventing further revolts.

The contest for Kyoto was fought by religious leaders as well as military captains. Some historians have felt that the greatest power in Kyoto in the first half of the century was wielded by Buddhist monks who took whichever side suited their purposes in any particular political quarrel. Many of the monasteries around Kyoto were notoriously corrupt, and the monks attached to them occupied themselves with drinking, gambling, fighting, and unconstrained licentiousness. In 1536, priests of the Hokke sect who, four years earlier, had driven out of Kyoto the monks of the Shin sect, were themselves attacked by monks from Hieisan. The great battle in the streets of the capital ended not only in the razing of all twenty-one Hokke temples, but half of rebuilt Kyoto was again burned. At the mercy of plundering armies and militant monks, the city was ravaged by floods and by epidemics of plague and smallpox. In July, 1544, the flooding Kamo River carried away the Shijo and Gojo bridges and even part of the imperial palace walls. The whole eastern portion of the city was under water, and this calamity, as might be expected, was followed by another epidemic. In the middle of the century, Kyoto was a capital city whose streets were lined with ruined buildings, where thousands of citizens lived in daily fear for their lives, and where learning, industry, and commerce were carried on under the most disheartening conditions.

Yet the citizen able to escape from the teeming streets

and miserable slums could find in less than an hour's walk into the surrounding hills quiet glades, rocky glens, gardens of enduring loveliness, and temples which were architectural masterpieces. If the Ashikaga were bad administrators, at least they had patronized a remarkable culture which was to have a profound influence on the Momoyama Period. Nowhere was Ashikaga taste more elegantly expressed than in several superb gardens and pavilions which survived into the sixteenth century. Gardens, of course, were less likely to be destroyed by burning and pillage. All of these spots were located in the foothills away from the center of the city, and as they belonged to temples, they were open to almost anyone who wanted to retreat to their peace and beauty. Women, unhappily, in some instances were barred from temple precincts.

The most ancient of these gardens was at Saiho-ji (1339), tucked away in a fold of the hills west of the city. Instead of the gay, sunny Heian garden with a large lake for boating, the Zen monk Muso Kokushi (1271–1346) had designed a quiet grove enclosing a winding pond of emerald green water. When many varieties of moss began to spread in the dim light under the trees, Saiho-ji became known as Koke-dera (Moss Temple). Yoshimitsu walked there on an autumn afternoon in 1380. His grandson, Yoshimasa, after his first visit in 1460, became the leader of a cult of admiration. Not far from the Moss Temple on the bank of the Oi River at Tenryu-ji was a second garden attributed to Kokushi. Like Saiho-ji it marked a turning away from the Heian pleasure park and foreshadowed the new, small Zen garden of simplicity and subtle symbolism. Its dry cascade composed of rocks in the style of a Chinese Sung landscape anticipated two strikingly conceived gardens of 150 years later which were to epitomize the spirit of Zen.

Perhaps the painter Soami (1472–1523) was the creator of the mysterious rock garden dating from about 1500 at Ryoan-ji. In an area about one hundred feet long and fifty feet wide enclosed by a veranda and earthen walls, fifteen stones are placed in five groups on coarse, raked sand. At first glance, these five groups appear to be distributed almost haphazardly. This impression of apparent artlessness is very deceptive, for there is an air of finality, almost of inevitability, about the arrangement. In this serene garden the essence and enigma of all Zen wisdom are blended. Since its rediscovery in the twentieth century, speculations about its meaning have been endless, but apparently no key exists from the period of its design.

At Daisen-in, part of the enormous Zen temple of Daitoku-ji, is a garden (c.1512) built around a single unusual rock, formerly belonging to Yoshimasa, which suggested a ship by its shape. A three-dimensional landscape in the style of Sung ink painting is fitted into an L-shaped space only a few feet wide. Stones were chosen which showed the same angular lines as brush strokes. In the northwest corner precipitous hills and cascades are formed of clipped shrubs and rocks. At the base of the dry cascades a river of gravel curves down among rocky gorges, the presence of water suggested by striated rocks and white sand flowing under stone bridges, between traditional "crane" and "tortoise" islands and over a rock dam. Possibly the stone boat resembling a Chinese junk represents the ship of life as it passes through the perils of the rocky stream. The gardens at Ryoan-ji and Daisen-in are both examples of *karesansui* ("lacking mountain and water"), a rock garden style which was to become extremely popular in the Momoyama Period.

Two elegant Ashikaga garden pavilions had also escaped

destruction. The Kinkaku (Gold Pavilion), set in a charming lake which was the scene of a splendid boating party when Yoshimitsu entertained Emperor Go Komatsu in 1408, had been built in 1397. The pavilion took its name from the fact that its Chinese style third story was covered inside and out with gold lacquer. A successful blending of Chinese and Japanese styles, the harmony and delicacy of its proportions were greatly admired by Momoyama architects. In 1488 Yoshimasa had completed the Ginkaku (Silver Pavilion) in imitation of his grandfather's Kinkaku.

Innovations in the Silver Pavilion which were to be significant in the next century included covering the entire ground floor with mats of rice straw (*tatami*) and dividing this area into rooms by sliding screens (*fusuma*). An adjacent thatched cottage, the Togu-do, built in 1486 as Yoshimasa's private chapel, held a small chamber about nine feet square which was the prototype of the classic tearoom. Perhaps planned by the Zen monk Shuko, Yoshimasa's tea master, this room was considered the birthplace of the tea ceremony. In the rear wall was an early version of the *tokonoma* ("space for a bed"), an alcove for the display of art treasures and floral arrangements. Alongside it was a *chigaidana*, a narrow recess crossed by ornamental shelves. Both the *tokonoma* and the *chigaidana* were to be incorporated in every Kyoto living room in the next century.

In the city itself two notable temples remained. One was the Sanjusangen-do (Thirty-three Spaces Hall) built in 1266 in southeastern Kyoto across the Kamo. In the center of this hall was an eight-foot golden statue of "Thousand-handed" Kannon flanked to right and left by hundreds of five-foot Kannon statues standing in tiers. These silent, many-armed, many-headed, golden figures, smiling inscrutably, created an atmosphere of pervasive mystery totally unlike that of any other temple in Kyoto. In the second half of the sixteenth century, it was one of the first places in the capital to which European sightseers were taken, and served to confirm the Christian view that the heathen Japanese were indeed devil-worshipers. The second temple was a great favorite with Japanese visitors as well as foreigners because from a platform in front of the central hall the entire city could be seen in one sweeping panorama. Kiyomizu-dera (Clear Water Temple) had been built on the Eastern Hills in the eighth century even before Kyoto was laid out, and for more than eight hundred years aristocrats and common folk alike had been climbing the hill in the spring to see the pink cherry blossoms in the ravine below or in the autumn for moon-viewing and scarlet maples. The temple was named for a sacred waterfall which plunged into a mossy pool in the deep shade of the glen. Hideyoshi was particularly fond of Kiyomizu and is said to have prayed there before making important decisions.

Even after the city had been rebuilt by Hideyoshi, Western visitors who climbed to the platform of Kiyomizu must have found the far-famed vista a disappointing one in comparison with views of the great cities of Europe. Kyoto had no broad paved squares, no majestic churches or council halls with soaring arches or classic colonnades, no domes or towers of brick and stone. It was essentially a city of low buildings constructed of unpainted, weathered wood and roofed with heavy gray tiles or brown thatch. The flat, horizontal effect of the city lying between the dark, pine-covered hills was relieved only occasionally by the gold and emerald tiles of Hideyoshi's palaces or the vermilion painted woodwork of a five-story pagoda. Yet to its citizens who looked down from Kiyomizu, the view recalled the vanished glories of magnificent Heian-kyo. The panorama of the city was softened by haze, giving it the appearance of a favorite Sung landscape, and in the moisture-laden atmosphere the roofs and hills shimmered with prismatic light of varied colors. Although its citizens might starve or its streets run red with the blood of religious sectarians, from Kiyomizu the capital appeared incomparably beautiful.

2

The Three Heroes

In 1551 at the time of Xavier's visit to Kyoto, it would have been impossible to predict that any of the several hundred warring daimyo could accomplish the unification of Japan. Nevertheless, within the final three decades of the century three remarkable men were able to bring the country into a new age, as significant for its peace and unity as the old one had been for its strife and chaos. These three military rulers who, by extraordinary chance, succeeded one another, were Oda Nobunaga (1534–82), Toyotomi Hideyoshi (1536–98) and Tokugawa Ieyasu (1542–1616).

During the thirty years between Nobunaga's triumphal entry into Kyoto in 1568 and the death of Hideyoshi in 1598, the imperial capital was the center of an unprecedented transformation of Japanese society. Peasants and serfs, freed from the land, flocked to the cities where they became artisans and merchants. Commerce and industry increased immeasurably. Religious life, no longer dominated by Buddhism, was diverted toward Confucian rationalism. Castles and palaces of unparalleled magnificence were constructed in Kyoto, Fushimi, Azuchi, and Osaka. There was an explosive outburst of brilliant color and bold design in painting, sculpture, ceramics, and weaving. It was a time of national glory and artistic achievement—the starting point for the history of modern Japan.

The story of Kyoto in those three decades is at the same time the story of the Three Heroes. Under the leadership of the second of these, Hideyoshi, the city reached the zenith of its prosperity and splendor. Through his conquests Nobunaga began the unification of Japan, Hideyoshi completed it, and Ieyasu established a strong feudal government which endured for more than 250 years. A cartoon of a later period shows Nobunaga pounding the rice for *mochi* (rice cake), Hideyoshi kneading the dough, and Ieyasu eating the cake. Katsuro Hara expressed the same idea more correctly when he wrote in his *Introduction to the History of Japan* (1920) that Nobunaga quarried the stones for a new Japan, Hideyoshi roughhewed them, and Ieyasu set them firmly in their proper place.

Halfway through the sixteenth century five great daimyo had grown so powerful they could begin to think of uniting all Japan. The immediate objective of several of these ambitious lords was to force their way through neighboring provinces, occupy Kyoto, and gain control of the Shogun and Emperor. Powerless as these two were, their assent was regarded as necessary to legalize the regional warfare which the daimyo were carrying on. The five great daimyo were formidable contestants, but there were many others including a very minor lord named Oda Nobunaga from the small province of Owari. Nobunaga was a product of the process which Japanese historians called *gekokujo*, the "overturning of those on top by those below." From obscure antecedents, Nobunaga's father, becoming assistant to the Deputy Governor of Owari, had made himself an influential lord in the province. When his father died in 1551, Nobunaga, then only seventeen years old, had to fight for ascendancy in the Oda family against his brother and other relatives. He was able to dispose of his hostile relatives, his brother was killed in the conflict, and by the age of twenty-five (1559) Nobunaga was the ruler of Owari.

It is true that Owari was a rather unimportant domain, but the personality of Nobunaga was not one to be contained within such restricted boundaries. He was well equipped for the ambitious task of destroying or reducing the autonomy of the five great daimyo, for he was bold, self-willed, ruthless, and ready to use the most deceitful strategems to accomplish his purposes. Showing his contempt for established tradition, he had appeared at his father's funeral without the customary mourning clothes and disdainfully tossed the incense on the corpse. This scorn for the conventional made him receptive to everything new. He was one of the first to recognize the importance of firearms which had been introduced into Japan by the Portuguese and is said to have organized the first company of infantry equipped with matchlocks. His later cordiality toward the Christian missionaries and the foreign traders seems to have been prompted by his curiosity to learn more about the industry and science of the western world. But above all he had a genius for military strategy and a notable gift for choosing the cleverest subordinates.

As Owari dominated the approaches to Kyoto from the north and east, Nobunaga was soon involved in strife. His first important step toward becoming master of Japan occurred in 1560 when one of the five daimyo, Imagawa, whose fief lay along the Pacific coast just east of Owari, set out for Kyoto with a force of 25,000 men. Imagawa had expected little resistance from his small neighbor, but on June 22, 1560, he was defeated and killed in the rocky defile of Okehazama by about 3,000 men under Nobunaga.

In the next few years with the aid of Kinoshita Tokichiro, who was to change his name to Toyotomi Hideyoshi and become an even greater military ruler than Nobunaga, all of the daimyo who blocked the road to Kyoto were defeated. Two years after the murder (or suicide) of the Shogun Yoshiteru in 1565 the Emperor Ogimachi sent secret instructions to Nobunaga asking him to occupy the city then in the hands of Matsunaga, an extremely unscrupulous and oppressive tyrant.

Not until November 9, 1568, did Nobunaga feel secure enough to enter Kyoto in a triumphal procession bringing Yoshiaki, the brother of Yoshiteru, to be installed as shogun with the blessing of Ogimachi. Upon Nobunaga's entrance, many citizens fled from the capital fearing that once again the city would be burned and looted. Happily, this proved not to be the case, for Nobunaga strictly prohibited his soldiers from plundering, issued orders to protect the safety of the people, and later persuaded merchants and artisans to return and set up their businesses. Hideyoshi, who was to prove a wise and efficient ruler, was made governor of the city. It was now more than seventeen years since the visit of Xavier to the capital. With the entrance of Nobunaga a new age began for Kyoto.

Several years before, Nobunaga had chosen "Rule the Empire by Force" as the motto to be engraved on his seal. He now made it obvious that he had no intention of subordinating himself to the Shogun. Their first quarrel occurred very shortly when Yoshiaki invited Nobunaga to be his guest at an elaborate No performance. After watching briefly, Nobunaga left, saying angrily that he had no leisure for such entertainment. He marched out of the city the next day and spent the remainder of 1568 subduing the two Gokinai provinces west of Kyoto. The following January he had to return to the capital when Matsunaga attacked Yoshiaki who was living at a temple on Rokujo (Sixth Avenue). Nobunaga rescued Yoshiaki and gave orders for rebuilding Nijo Palace for the Shogun and the Tsuchi-mikado Palace for the Emperor. These projects increased Nobunaga's popularity with the citizens of Kyoto, for all of the other military rulers had treated the Shogun and Emperor with disrespect. Again Nobunaga's stay in the capital was short because he still held only about a dozen provinces out of a total of sixty-six in Japan. In April, 1569, he was back in Kyoto supervising the erection of Nijo Palace. He took a great interest in the construction of this new residence for the Shogun, now shouting directions from a place on the scaffolding, now striding about the garden in his rough clothing girded about with a tiger-skin showing workmen where to place bushes and trees. Father Luis Frois, one of the Jesuit missionaries in Kyoto who was presented to Nobunaga at this time, has left the following account of this meeting:

> He would be about thirty-seven years old, a tall man, lean, scantily bearded, with a clear voice, greatly addicted to military exercises, hardy, disposed to temper justice with mercy, proud, a great stickler for honor, very secretive in his plans, most expert in the wiles of warfare, little or nothing disposed to accept reproof or advice from his subordinates, but greatly feared and respected by everyone. He does not drink wine, he is rough mannered, contemptuous of all the other kings and nobles of Japan whom he addresses brusquely over his shoulder as if they were inferiors, while he is punctiliously obeyed by all as their complete master. He is of good understanding and clear judgment, despising both Shinto and Buddhist deities and all other

forms of idolatry and superstition. . . . Extremely refined and clean in his dress and in the nobility of his actions; annoyed at anybody who addresses him hesitantly or with circumlocution; not even a prince dare appear before him with a sword; he is always attended by a train of at least two thousand pages on horseback.

During the construction of Nijo, Nobunaga had several nearby monasteries dismantled to make use of their materials, and the supply of stone running short, he ordered all the stone statues in Kyoto broken up. The missionaries were delighted to see various Buddhist gods being dragged through the streets with ropes around their necks. When the new imperial palace was finished (1571), for the first time in a century the imperial family had satisfactory living quarters. As more than 25,000 workmen were brought into Kyoto from conquered provinces to labor on these projects, the problems of feeding and housing them in the partially rebuilt city were enormous. The lack of food and shelter, the forced labor, and the prevalence of disease caused the deaths of thousands.

With the possible exception of the Zen sect, Nobunaga was known to hate the Buddhists with a stubborn vindictiveness, but it was generally considered that the sacredness of the ancient Hieisan temples northeast of the city would give even Nobunaga pause. Nevertheless, early in October, 1571, he ordered his troops to storm Hieisan. All the historic buildings with their priceless art treasures were set on fire, and more than 3,000 monks, women, and children were captured and beheaded. Nobunaga evidently intended this massacre as a warning that he would not be lenient with any further political interference by the Buddhist clergy. He was further exasperated by the plots and intrigues revolving around Yoshiaki and finally sent the Shogun a long letter of complaint. At last in July, 1573, he attacked Nijo, but Yoshiaki escaped. The flight of the Shogun to western Japan brought to a close the Ashikaga shogunate after 230 years. Although Yoshiaki lived until 1597 and made various attempts to regain his position, he was never able to do so. Thus the office of shogun remained vacant for thirty years, from 1573 until 1603, when Ieyasu, who claimed descent from the Minamoto family, had himself appointed.

In the next few years Nobunaga spent as much time on administrative matters in Kyoto as he could afford away from campaigning in the provinces. When he was in the city, he made his headquarters at the Chion-in, a large monastery on the lower slopes of Higashiyama between Sanjo and Shijo. He did not choose to live in Kyoto because experience had shown that a fortress inside the city was a disadvantage and, indeed, a danger. The risk of fire was constant, and the capital was too flat and sprawling to serve as a military base. Even in 1573 much of Kyoto was still deserted, according to a letter written by the Jesuit missionary, Father Organtino, to his superiors. Nobunaga had presented the Jesuits with a lot on which to build a church, and Father Organtino reported that the land, although in the center of the city, was surrounded by open fields. After the palaces for the Shogun and Emperor were completed, Nobunaga decided to build a castle for himself. He selected a site on a six-hundred-foot high promontory rising above the shore of Lake Biwa at Azuchi, twenty miles east of Kyoto. There between 1576 and 1579 a vast complex of walls, mansions, and towers was erected.

To entertain Ieyasu who was visiting Kyoto in the late spring of 1582, Nobunaga asked Akechi Mitsuhide, one of his generals, to prepare an elaborate banquet. Akechi, who had come into Nobunaga's service as a *ronin*, or warrior without a master, had impressed Nobunaga with his talents to such an extent that he held a rank equal with Hideyoshi. Nobunaga seems to have had no idea that Akechi was planning his assassination. One story relates that Nobunaga insulted Akechi at Ieyasu's banquet by shouting that the food was unclean and kicking over the tables. A second version has it that Ieyasu failed to appear for the banquet on two occasions, and when Akechi complained to Nobunaga, the latter beat him over the head with a heavy iron fan. More probably Akechi attacked Nobunaga because he thought he could take possession of Kyoto and make himself the military ruler of Japan.

Akechi seized an opportunity for the assassination when Hideyoshi was away from Kyoto campaigning in western Japan against Mori, one of the two of the five great daimyo still undefeated. When it appeared that Mori's castle of Takamatsu was about to fall, Hideyoshi tactfully suggested that Nobunaga should be present for the capture. The latter left his castle at Azuchi with fewer than a hundred men instead of the guard of two thousand who usually traveled with him, and took up quarters in Kyoto at the Honno-ji, a protected monastery residence. By chance the Jesuit church was situated only one street away from the Honno-ji, and the Jesuit fathers witnessed the turmoil in the early morning of June 21, 1582, when Akechi's men attacked the monastery. Nobunaga fought bravely but was shot with an arrow and either committed *seppuku* or was burned to death when the building was set on fire. Except for the Honno-ji and some damage to Nijo, nothing in Kyoto was destroyed. When the news of Nobunaga's death reached Hideyoshi, he kept it a secret and quickly arranged for the surrender of Takamatsu. With a few retainers he hurried back to Kyoto from western Japan, assembled loyal troops, and on June 30 defeated Akechi about eight miles southwest of the city at Yamazaki on the Katsura River. Akechi fled, was wounded by a peasant, and then killed himself. The Buddhists were not hesitant in announcing that Nobunaga's assassination was an appropriate reward for the violence with which he had treated the clergy.

At his death Nobunaga was master of about half of the Japanese provinces—all of them centrally grouped within a radius of 150 miles of Kyoto. Most judgments of his character are highly unfavorable. He was courageous and determined, but he was also a brutal and tyrannical conqueror who never showed a sign of compassion for the victims he treated with appalling cruelty. If he seemed more vicious than Hideyoshi or Ieyasu, it is perhaps because they ruled in more settled times. In justice to Nobunaga, it should be pointed out that whatever his character, his achievements in unifying central Japan were notable. He brought peace to Kyoto for the first time in centuries, he built palaces for the Shogun and Emperor and did much to restore respect for the imperial house, he encouraged the resumption of agriculture in the surrounding region, and he pulled down the toll barriers which prevented trade from flowing into the city. A new class of wealthy merchants centered their businesses in Kyoto because of his gold coinage policies and his recognition of the importance of overseas trade with Europe and the Asiatic continent. Most important of all, by his conquests he laid the foundations for Hideyoshi and Ieyasu to raise the structure of a stable national government. Nobunaga's life furnished a fitting prelude to the Momoyama Period as a time of hope and freedom when vigorous men of strong will and natural ability could push their way upward no matter what their family antecedents.

Nobunaga had been the father of at least twelve sons and eleven daughters, but none of his descendants was strong enough to succeed him. When Hideyoshi came to Kyoto in November, 1582, for the funeral services for Nobunaga at the Daitoku-ji, he made it very clear to the principal daimyo that he had no intention of allowing anyone but himself to assume the leadership of Japan. He had the entire temple surrounded by his own troops and gave himself a more prominent place in the ceremonies than even Nobunaga's sons had. Within two years Hideyoshi's power was greater than that of his former master ever had been. He was fortunate in becoming Nobunaga's successor at the beginning of a golden age of commercial prosperity and artistic accomplishment. This expanding prosperity of a Japan emerging from the chaos of feudal warfare seems to have come about rather paradoxically because the regional daimyo had needed to produce enough wealth to carry on their increasingly expensive wars of conquest. By improving agricultural methods, opening up mines, and promoting trade and industry, the daimyo financed their battles and at the same time helped the country to move out of the restricted feudal economy of previous centuries. It was also a happy circumstance for Japan that Hideyoshi was able to assume command, for it seems likely that otherwise all Nobunaga had achieved toward establishing a strong central government would have been wasted.

Hideyoshi was born in 1536 in the village of Nakamura in that same small province of Owari where the young Nobunaga had become daimyo in 1559. He was the son of Yaemon, a peasant who had been a foot soldier in the service of Nobunaga's father. As a young boy, Hideyoshi seemed to have no attractive or promising qualities. Placed as a servant in a neighboring temple, he made his escape from there at the age of fifteen and entered the service of the warden of Kuno Castle. According to legend, when the latter gave him six *ryo* to purchase a new coat of mail for his master, Hideyoshi took the money, bought clothes and weapons for himself, and ran away to seek employment with Nobunaga. Although lacking education, Hideyoshi possessed an extraordinary intuitive knowledge of human nature and an amazing ability as a military commander. These talents were soon recognized, and he quickly became Nobunaga's most trusted general. In 1582 he was forty-six years old, scarcely five feet tall, with a dark complexion and a face said to resemble that of a wizened ape. According to a Korean embassy report, he was "mean and ignoble, but his eyeballs sent out fire in flashes–enough to pierce one through."

When he assumed command, three large regions of the country still refused to acknowledge the suzerainty of Kyoto. These were the two islands of Shikoku and Kyushu in western Japan and the whole area of Honshu, the main island, north of Odawara. The route to the Kanto ("east of the barrier"), the fertile plain around modern Tokyo, was blocked by Hojo, the last of the five great daimyo who had once been a threat to Nobunaga. Like the latter, Hideyoshi decided that he must build himself a strongly fortified castle outside the capital. Azuchi was not available, as it had been burned with all its resplendent interior decorations at the period of Nobunaga's death.

When Hideyoshi had beseiged Osaka in 1580, he had realized how valuable the location was, and in 1583 he began to build an enormous castle there. It was incomparably greater than Azuchi with an outer courtyard eight miles in circumference. Tens of thousands of workmen were employed in its construction. The commercial importance of

Osaka, eventually to overshadow Kyoto as a trade center, dates from the erection of Hideyoshi's castle. By 1584 Hideyoshi had dismantled almost all the forts around Kyoto which might shelter foes making an assault on the city. When in the following year the chief daimyo of Shikoku was subdued, Hideyoshi became the lord of almost half Japan. Now only Kyushu, the Kanto, and northern Honshu remained outside his control.

Whenever affairs required his presence in Kyoto, he stayed at the temple of the Daitoku-ji or at the house of Ito Ryoton in Sanjo between Muromachi and Shinmachi. He began to feel so secure in the capital that in the spring of 1585 he decided to build himself a palatial mansion. The Jurakudai (Palace of Pleasure), as this enormous palace was called, was spread over an area of one-half mile from north to south between Ichijo and Shijo on part of what had been the original Heian imperial palace enclosure. During 1585 Hideyoshi was made kampaku, regent for the emperor, although he would have preferred to become shogun. But even Hideyoshi dared not make himself shogun in defiance of the tradition that only descendants of the Minamoto family could assume that office. The next year, however, he took the family name Toyotomi ("Abundant Provider"), implying a relationship with the Fujiwaras who had held the office of kampaku for two centuries during the Heian period.

Hideyoshi's strongest rival occupying a fief near Kyoto was Ieyasu. Well aware that he could not capture Kyoto from Hideyoshi, Ieyasu also knew, as did Hideyoshi, that he could hold his own provinces against all comers. Early in 1585, Hideyoshi, who was noted for his clever diplomacy, devised several schemes which were intended to insure peace with Ieyasu. He invited him to visit Kyoto, but when Ieyasu refused to come, Hideyoshi adopted Ieyasu's eleven-year-old son in an elaborately staged public ceremony. Next, Hideyoshi divorced his half-sister Asahi-hime from her husband and gave her in marriage to Ieyasu. Then in September Hideyoshi suggested that his mother, to whom he was dearly devoted, should pay a visit to her daughter and Ieyasu, thus becoming a hostage while Ieyasu traveled to Kyoto. Ieyasu's ceremonial visit took place with expressions of the deepest friendship and passed without any unfortunate incidents, although he had made plans before leaving home as to what was to be done if Hideyoshi attempted any treachery.

In 1586–87 Hideyoshi was away from the capital much of the time, busy with the subjugation of Kyushu, but in Kyoto another enormous building project was under way. He had decided to erect a temple containing a Great Buddha (Daibutsu) larger than the eighth-century bronze at Nara, which was fifty-three feet high, or the similar statue at Kamakura (1252), forty-two feet tall, not because he was a pious Buddhist but because it was an opportunity to impress the country with his wealth and power. Over a period of five or six years, several hundred thousand laborers were brought to Kyoto to work on this immense edifice. All of Hideyoshi's vassals were required to furnish these workers and to bear the actual cost of construction. He also made use of the erection of the Daibutsu to disarm the farmers, monks, merchants, and artisans. Everyone except the warriors was forbidden to possess swords of any kind. Later known as the Taiko's Sword Hunt, this measure was intended not only to prevent insurrections but also to emphasize the class distinction between the samurai and all the other classes. The confiscated arms were melted into nails and bolts for building the hall of the Daibutsu.

After the conquest of Kyushu, Hideyoshi returned to Osaka, and from there in October, 1587, he moved to the newly completed Jurakudai with 5,000 wagons and 5,000 porters carrying gold, silver, and furnishings. The road all the way from Yodo into the city was lined with people who had come to see this great procession. As he now had a Kyoto palace worthy of entertaining the Emperor, the newly enthroned Go Yozei was soon invited to be Hideyoshi's guest at Jurakudai. On the day of the Emperor's visit, the mile-long road from the imperial palace to the Jurakudai was lined with 6,000 lavishly costumed troops. The Emperor's procession was so long that when the first palanquins of the princes, *kuge*, and ministers had reached Hideyoshi's mansion, the imperial oxcart had not yet left the palace enclosure. Immense crowds thronged the city, for an imperial progress had not taken place for more than a century. The real purpose of this entertainment was shown on the second day when the daimyo were asked to take a written oath to protect the estates of the crown and nobles and to obey the commands of Hideyoshi. The Emperor enjoyed himself so much he stayed five days and later invited Hideyoshi to the palace.

By 1589 Hideyoshi had an annual income of 2,000,000 *koku*, and about a year after the Emperor's visit, some of the most important court nobles and daimyo, including Ieyasu, were asked to another splendid entertainment. When they arrived, they found piled up on trays in the inner gallery of the Jurakudai 365,000 *ryo* in gold and silver pieces which Hideyoshi then proceeded to distribute among his guests. After his victory in Kyushu (1587), the only serious threat to his power, aside from Ieyasu whom he always treated with special consideration, was the Hojo family which ruled the Kanto from their castle at Odawara.

When Hojo Ujimasa refused to come to Kyoto in 1589 to pay homage to the Emperor, Hideyoshi marched a huge force of 200,000 men to Odawara, destroyed the castle (1590), and killed the leading members of the Hojo family. With the submission of Date Masamune of Sendai in northeastern Japan, Hideyoshi was at last the ruler of a united nation.

Hideyoshi's only child, Tsurumatsu, died in 1591 at the age of three. Although rumor reported that when Hideyoshi campaigned in the provinces, all of the beautiful girls in the vicinity were requisitioned for the Kampaku's nightly pleasures, he had had no children until the birth of his son. The mother of Tsurumatsu was his lovely young mistress Yodogimi, whom he had not met until he was already forty-eight years old. Whether Hideyoshi was Tsurumatsu's father was a whispered question around his court, although he himself was convinced of Yodogimi's virtue. Left without an heir, he adopted his sister's child, Hidetsugu, who was then twenty years old. Hidetsugu was appointed kampaku, and Hideyoshi became the taiko, a title reserved for retired regents. As the Jurakudai was given to Hidetsugu for his Kyoto residence, Hideyoshi began to plan a new castle at Fushimi, about three miles south of the city in a beautiful valley which for centuries had been a favorite summer resort of the Kyoto nobility. The site of the castle, overlooking the Uji River, commanded a strategic position from the hill later known as Momoyama. Every lord in northeastern Japan who had an income of 10,000 *koku* was ordered to send laborers. Since the end of the civil wars had caused unemployment among both warriors and artisans, this plan was a method of keeping the lower classes busy and reducing the wealth of the daimyo.

While the lords from northeastern Japan were building

Fushimi, those in southwestern Japan were being taxed to finance and supply an expedition to conquer Korea. There is no agreement about Hideyoshi's purpose in invading the Asiatic mainland. Some Japanese historians believe his success in forcing Japanese society into a single pattern by such methods as his land registration and Sword Hunt had caused so much discontent that it was a means of preventing revolts in Japan itself. Obviously Hideyoshi did not realize the size of China which he planned to attack after victory in Korea.

In September, 1593, while he was in Kyushu directing the embarkation for Korea, Yodogimi gave birth to a second son. Hideyoshi was so overjoyed at the arrival of Hideyori, which was the name given to the baby, that his retainers could scarcely believe that the father lavishing kisses on the tiny child and the bold warrior who was the master of Japan were the same person. As Hideyoshi had been away from Yodogimi most of the previous year, there were those who hinted in secret that he was not really the father. Subsequent events were to suggest that there were grounds for such gossip.

After 1593 for the last five years of his life Hideyoshi spent an increasing part of his time with aesthetic activities, entertaining and visiting great lords, attending No performances, and supervising his building projects. A sumptuous banquet was staged in 1595 to mark the completion of his surrender of power as kampaku to Hidetsugu. Thereupon his nephew tendered him an equally splendid feast at the Jurakudai, but at the last moment Hideyoshi sent word he was unable to attend. According to Frois, Hidetsugu had a noble presence, an engaging manner, a love for the fine arts, and "one weakness, namely a passionate delight in killing." Whether Hideyoshi felt that his nephew's conduct made him unsuitable as the future ruler of Japan, or whether he feared that after his own death Hidetsugu would murder Yodogimi and his young son Hideyori is not certain. In any case, Hideyoshi surrounded Kyoto with troops and then wrote to Hidetsugu accusing him of plotting to capture Osaka Castle. When Hidetsugu went to Fushimi in abject submission, his uncle refused to see him and ordered his retirement to a monastery on Koyasan. Upon his arrival there, he was met by messengers sent by Hideyoshi commanding him to commit *seppuku*. Shortly afterward thirty-one women from Hidetsugu's household together with his three young children were dragged through the streets of Kyoto and executed at Sanjomachi. Their bodies were thrown into a pit with Hidetsugu's son and heir at the very bottom and the corpses covered by a great mound. This relentless extermination of Hidetsugu and his family was so unlike Hideyoshi's usual policy of clemency that Ieyasu did not hesitate to rebuke him for it. Hideyoshi ordered the Jurakudai razed in September, 1595, and every building associated with Hidetsugu's memory destroyed.

No agreement with China had been reached following the Korean invasion of 1592–93, until in 1596 Hideyoshi received word that at last a mission from the Chinese Ming emperor was to arrive in Japan. Lavish preparations were made at Fushimi for this visit. Mounted warriors in armor were to line both sides of the road from Yawata, about seven miles south, to the main entrance of the castle, but three days before a preliminary drill of these warriors was to take place, a succession of disastrous earthquakes occurred in Kyoto and its vicinity. All of Hideyoshi's buildings in Kyoto were severely damaged; the Daibutsu, completed only seven years before, was toppled over; and at Fushimi the castle was shaken down and four hundred people killed. Hideyoshi and his lords, who had been living at Fushimi in thatched huts, were not injured. The earthquake damage was quickly repaired, and in December, 1596, the Chinese mission was received with extravagant magnificence. When the Chinese read a very patronizing letter from the Ming court, Hideyoshi burst into a rage and insulted the envoys. Dismissing them with expensive gifts, he declared his intention of continuing the war. An invasion force of 100,000 men was sent to Korea the following March.

In the spring of 1598 Hideyoshi, his six or seven consorts, and a group of nobles went to the village of Daigo, near Fushimi, to view the famous cherry blossoms. He seems not to have been well during this visit, and at Fushimi toward the end of June, 1598, he had an attack of what may have been dysentery. When it became obvious that his condition was critical, the five daimyo whose influence and military power were the greatest in the nation met and exchanged oaths to be loyal to Hideyoshi's young son Hideyori, to obey Hideyoshi's laws, and not to pursue their own private purposes. Of the five, Ieyasu with an income of 2,500,000 *koku* was the most powerful, ruling the greater part of the Kanto from his newly built fortress-town of Edo. In his testament drawn up by his physician, Hideyoshi asked Ieyasu to be the guardian of Hideyori and regent until the young boy was fifteen. Ieyasu was to occupy Fushimi in general control of the country, and Hideyori was to live at Osaka with his mother Yodogimi. Hideyoshi did everything he could to assure the continuance of the house of Toyotomi.

On September 11 he wrote a farewell in *kana* script, "It is sad to part from you," and then lingered on for several days, his mind wandering. He died September 18, 1598, in his sixty-third year. "It is usually agreed," wrote Sir George Sansom in his *History of Japan, 1334–1615*, "that Hideyoshi is the greatest man in the history of Japan," an opinion which is shared by most Japanese historians. The agreement on his military ability and political achievements is very nearly unanimous. He had courage, adaptability, a shrewd knowledge of human nature, frankness, and generosity. As a commander he always tried to avoid killing men in battle if he could win by any other means and, unlike Nobunaga, dealt liberally with those he defeated. Along with his affectionate nature, he had a strong sense of duty to his family and friends. His vengeance on Hidetsugu's family was so unbelievably cruel, and much of his behavior in the final years of his life so erratic that Sansom has raised the question of whether Hideyoshi was deranged after about 1592.

Hideyoshi was indeed fortunate in living in a period when the growth of commerce and manufacturing, the spread of money economy, and the extension of overseas trade made possible his vast building projects and spectacular entertainments. Although he may have been almost illiterate, he surrounded himself with the greatest scholars, architects, and artists of the period. His delight in ostentatious display, which resulted in great works of art and architecture, can doubtless be partly attributed to his peasant origin. By the standards of the age he was a talented and successful ruler, but he was at the same time a greedy despot ruling by terror, who never used his unprecedented wealth and power to achieve a more democratic form of government. Through his struggles to bring all of Japan under his authority, he actually strengthened the feudal system. Many men of ability, whether samurai, merchants, farmers, or artisans, had been allowed by the unsettled conditions of the Momoyama Period to develop their best faculties and to move rather freely from one class to another. Unfortunately, his prohibitions on carrying arms or changing residence and employment had the effect of creating a rigid caste system and a new feudal hierarchy.

The imperial court took the lead in expressing the people's reverence for Hideyoshi by raising a shrine on the southeastern hills and granting him a Shinto title. The temple where he was buried became such a center of national hero-worship that the Tokugawa shoguns took steps to destroy some of his memorials. By the time of the publication in 1625 of the *Taikoki*, a biography of the Taiko in twenty-one volumes by an anonymous author, his life had already acquired a legendary quality. He was to remain Japan's greatest hero, the only peasant boy who became the nation's ruler.

Immediately after Hideyoshi's death, Ieyasu moved into the castle at Fushimi. With the first ruler from the Tokugawa family, another age begins; an age of disorderly splendor and democratic promise had ended. Ieyasu was the eldest son of a minor war lord named Matsudaira whose lands lay in Mikawa Province near those of Nobunaga's family in Owari. Ieyasu was born in 1542 at Okazaki, about twenty miles southeast of modern Nagoya, the year of his birth perhaps that fateful one when Europeans first landed in Japan. In 1560 when Nobunaga began his rise to power by defeating Imagawa Yoshimoto at Okehazama, Ieyasu was present at the battle on the Imagawa side. The year following he became a vassal of Nobunaga, and by 1568 when Nobunaga occupied Kyoto, he was the ruler of the province of Mikawa. He continued to support Nobunaga but after the latter's death showed little indication of wanting to overthrow Hideyoshi.

Ieyasu was fifty-six years old when Hideyoshi died in 1598. Short, powerfully built, and far from distinguished in appearance, he was rather blunt and cold by nature, sometimes seeming almost inhuman in his lack of emotion. Although he went to poetry contests, attended and even performed in No plays, and took part in the tea ceremony, his only real recreation was hawking. He was said to have looked like a true war god when hawking and was as fond of his hawks as Hideyoshi was of his extravagant mansions. Loving simplicity and economy, he was content to live in a modest style. More than either Nobunaga or Hideyoshi, he appeared to be an average man, but in reality he seems to have been less candid and honest in his dealings with rivals and friends than Hideyoshi.

The first important act of the Tairo, the five chief regents, in the autumn of Hideyoshi's death was to withdraw the troops from Korea. About November the Japanese had won a great victory, and the noses of 38,000 Korean soldiers had been sliced off, pickled in tubs, and sent to Kyoto where they were interred in the Mimi-zuka, or so-called Ear Mound. Ieyasu soon found that his most unrelenting enemy was the clever, ambitious *Bugyo,* Ishida Mitsunari, who had been a favorite of Hideyoshi. Mitsunari schemed to cause a quarrel between Ieyasu and Maeda Toshi-ie, the guardian of Hideyori, but Toshi-ie died in May, 1599. Ieyasu presently gave the other members of the Tairo cause for complaint when, without consulting them, he made several political marriages for his sons and daughters.

The first open revolt against him was begun by one of the Tairo, Uyesugi, in the region north of Edo. In May, 1600, Ieyasu marched north from Fushimi to confront Uyesugi. While there he received word that his return route to Kyoto was barred by the troops of a western confederation which included two other Tairo and Mitsunari. Leading from Kyoto to Edo were two highways, the Tokaido, the road along the Pacific, and the Nakasendo, which led through the mountains. At Miya in Owari these two roads were only twenty miles apart. By September the armies of the western confederation and the Tokugawa allies faced each other across this distance. On October 21, 1600, the two armies met in fog and rain near the village of Sekigahara on the Nakasendo. Partly owing to treachery in the western army, Ieyasu's victory was overwhelming. Mitsunari and two other leaders were decapitated at the public execution grounds at Sanjomachi in Kyoto. To maintain peace, Ieyasu distributed confiscated fiefs to trusted vassals known as Fudai in such a way that they could block the expansion of the Tozama, or "outside" daimyo, who were not related to the Tokugawa family. Ieyasu was now the undisputed ruler of Japan, but he was careful not to suggest that he intended to displace Hideyori and wise enough not to raise the issue of succession.

Shortly after his victory at Sekigahara, Ieyasu and his son Hidetada held a conference at Osaka on whether the seat of their government should be in Kyoto or Edo. After a long and earnest discussion, they decided to keep Edo as their capital. Ieyasu did not enjoy the cultural pursuits for which Kyoto was renowned and feared the enervating influence of the imperial court on the shoguns, which had been illustrated all too clearly by the decline of the Ashikaga. Like Nobunaga and Hideyoshi, Ieyasu was an outsider in the capital. Kyoto men were hereditary courtiers, priests, artists, scholars, or merchants, and Ieyasu who had spent his life as a warrior had little in common with any of them. He was always suspicious of everyone who had lived for any length of time in Kyoto. Hideyoshi had considered himself as one of the court nobles; he ruled through the military government, but he looked on the Emperor as his lord. Ieyasu regarded himself as the military administrator of the nation with the imperial court in a completely subordinate position.

After his meeting with Hidetada, Ieyasu returned to Fushimi where he had the castle, which had been burned by Mitsunari's troops, rebuilt and occupied by a permanent garrison. He did not rebuild the mansion but had some old timbers collected and put up a rough residence which amused the people of Kyoto who regarded it as just another example of his parsimony. Within the capital he began construction in 1602 on Nijo Castle on the site of the palace erected by Nobunaga in 1569 for the last Ashikaga shogun. For thirty years there had been no shogun since the deposition of Yoshiaki in 1573. As Ieyasu claimed to be a descendant of the house of Minamoto, he was eligible for the shogunate and therefore had himself appointed in 1603, becoming the first of the Tokugawas, a name taken from the place where Ieyasu's reputed Minamoto ancestors had lived at the beginning of the thirteenth century. Having built Nijo as headquarters for the *Shoshidai*, the Governor of Kyoto, Ieyasu stayed there himself at the time of his appointment as shogun. Although Nijo was luxuriously furnished to impress visiting daimyo, Ieyasu lived very simply in one room and ate only rough soldier's fare of rice, fish, and pickled radishes. Edo was officially established as the military capital when he went to reside there in 1603 upon assuming office as shogun.

Aware that neither Nobunaga nor Hideyoshi had been able to keep the succession in their families, Ieyasu was determined to see the Tokugawa family so strongly established that the ruling power would pass on to his descendants. In 1605 he resigned as shogun in favor of his son Hidetada, but although retired to his home province, he actually continued to control the government. Hidetada, twenty-six years old in 1605, was well qualified to carry on his father's policies, for he was cautious, calculating, and patient; moreover, he had always before him the fate of Hidetsugu. Kyoto was once more honored with the presence of a Tokugawa when Hidetada appeared at Fushimi accompanied by an army of 70,000 and then went on to the capital to be confirmed as shogun by the Emperor. After 1603, Ieyasu did not return to Kyoto for eight years. His next recorded visit was not until April 30, 1611, when he arrived in the city with 60,000 men and invited Hideyori to visit him at Nijo. Hideyori was understandably reluctant to leave the safety of Osaka Castle, but he finally agreed and was conducted with great pomp to Nijo where a banquet had been prepared. Katagiri Katsumoto, who had become Hideyori's guardian, had given out that his charge was dull and incapable. Unfortunately for Hideyori, Ieyasu, impressed by his handsome appearance and apparent wisdom, decided that he was a menace to the Tokugawa family and must be dealt with as soon as possible. Ieyasu returned to Edo shortly afterward and did not set foot in Kyoto again until his final conflict with Hideyori.

To prevent Hideyori and his mother, Yodogimi, from using for military purposes the large quantities of gold left by Hideyoshi, Ieyasu persuaded them to melt down ten million gold coins for a gigantic image replacing the Daibutsu destroyed in the 1596 earthquake. In 1612 a new temple for the Daibutsu was completed, and only the casting of a magnificent bell remained. By April, 1614, a bell more than fourteen feet tall and weighing over sixty-three tons was finished. Several days before the consecration of the temple in August, 1614, Katagiri Katsumoto, who was supervising the reconstruction, was informed that Ieyasu had taken offense at the inscription on the bell. This inscription in Chinese ideograms read "*Kokka Anko*" or "May the state be peaceful and prosperous." "*Ka*" and "*ko*" can also be read as "*Ie*" and "*yasu*," and since they happened to be just at the point where the bell was struck, these symbols were interpreted as putting a curse on Ieyasu. Katagiri and Seikan, the priest who had written the inscription, sought an audience with Ieyasu but were refused. The four offending characters were scraped off the bell, but it was clear to Hideyori's supporters that Ieyasu had resolved to destroy the house of Toyotomi.

Ono Harunaga who was probably the lover of Yodogimi, and possibly Hideyori's actual father, wanted to seize Fushimi Castle and burn Kyoto. Many of the citizens fled from the capital, but instead of attacking Kyoto, Hideyori began to prepare Osaka Castle for a siege. He recruited thousands of defenders who were *ronin*, masterless warriors who had lost their property after the battle of Sekigahara. In November, 1614, Ieyasu reached Kyoto and quartered at Nijo. From there he set out with Hidetada and 70,000 men to besiege Osaka. When it became apparent that as long as the defenders were united, the castle was impregnable, Ieyasu made peace proposals. Why Hideyori accepted a peace agreement allowing the outer defenses of the castle to be demolished is not known. The Winter Siege (*Fuyu no Jin*) was thus ended on January 21, 1615; Ieyasu left for home, and Hidetada immediately began to pull down the outer walls of Osaka and fill up the moats. On May 20, 1615, Ieyasu was back in Kyoto at Nijo and was joined there by Hidetada. A few days later they began the Summer Siege (*Natsu no Jin*) in which there were as many as 100,000 defenders and 200,000 attackers. On June 3 the attackers entered Osaka; the next day Hideyori committed suicide, and Yodogimi was killed by a retainer. Ieyasu ordered the murder of Hideyori's little son and an unsparing extermination of everyone connected with the house of Toyotomi. Plainly he considered this savage massacre the only safe guarantee for a permanent peace. In contrast to the fleeting domination of Nobunaga and Hideyoshi, the Tokugawa family was to govern for more than 250 years.

Ieyasu was now supreme in Japan, and without delay he summoned all the leading daimyo to Kyoto. After a great banquet at Nijo for the victorious generals, the daimyo were commanded to attend a meeting at Fushimi to hear the promulgation of two codes for the guidance of the aristocracy and the military class. During the Osaka campaign Ieyasu had been in Kyoto borrowing the records of the imperial court and gathering books and manuscripts from noble families so that he might examine precedents for the two ordinances he was about to issue. The first code, called the *Kuge Sho-Hatto* listed seventeen regulations limiting the activities of the imperial court. The second was a collection of rules known as the *Buke Sho-Hatto* or Ordinances for the Military Houses. They were not a code of laws but statements compiled from various sources to govern the conduct of the daimyo. "Archery and horsemanship," declared the first article, "are indispensable to military men"; the second forbade licentious habits; and others warned against privately arranged marriages or repairing castles without permission. Notwithstanding the promulgation of these ordinances, Ieyasu made no definite attempt to set up a systematic form of government. The political system which he handed on to his Tokugawa successors contained little that was new and much that was derived from Hideyoshi. After Ieyasu a very rigid form of government was developed. Life in Kyoto and all of Japan was to be severely regulated by the Tokugawa Bakufu; the social mobility and economic freedom of the sixteenth century were brought to an abrupt end.

Ieyasu died on June 1, 1616, in his seventy-fifth year as he was in the midst of arranging details for his deification. It was indicative of the declining importance of Kyoto that his pretentiously overdecorated shrine was erected not in the imperial capital but at Nikko, in the mountains ninety miles north of Edo. The posthumous title chosen for Ieyasu as first of the Tokugawa line was Tosho Gongen, "Buddha Incarnate as the Sun God of the East." The differing characters of the Three Heroes of the Momoyama Period are well illustrated by some verses about a cuckoo who refused to sing. Nobunaga is supposed to have declared, "I'll kill the cuckoo, if it won't sing." Hideyoshi, who was less cruel and less headstrong, said, "I shall invite it to sing." Ieyasu, always the clever diplomat, observed, "I'll wait until the cuckoo does sing."

3

Rakuchu, or Within the Capital

In 1591 Hideyoshi ordered the construction of the Odoi (Great Rampart), an earthen wall thirty-five feet high which extended seventeen miles around the city. Although built for defensive purposes, this wall reminded the scholars that in Heian times a purely ornamental wall copied from the Chinese Sui Dynasty capital of Ch'ang-an had surrounded Kyoto. Since gentlemen of fashion who hoped to give an impression of classical learning delighted in referring to Kyoto by the Chinese ideogram Raku (capital), everything within the enclosure of the Odoi became known as Rakuchu, "within the capital," and everything beyond as Rakugai, "outside the capital." The Odoi in 1591 enclosed a population estimated at about 500,000 people, making Kyoto the largest city in the world except possibly Paris. As Fushimi, Osaka, and Sakai were all large cities by the end of the century, another 400,000 people lived within a forty-mile circle. Japan contained at least eighteen million inhabitants at a time when Elizabethan England had a population of only four and one-half million, Spain eight million, and France fourteen million.

A letter from Father Vilela twenty years earlier in October, 1571, noted that the capital then had 60,000 houses out of 300,000 it had reputedly numbered before the Onin War. Perhaps the population had decreased by 1571 as low as 250,000, but it was surely larger than it had been twenty years before that in 1551 when Xavier had visited the city. About the time of Vilela's letter a survey ordered by Nobunaga listed only 127 *cho*, or blocks of houses, compared with 1,126 *cho* in early Heian times. By 1634 the number of *cho* had increased to 1,279. The population, however, reached its height about the turn of the century and was known to have dropped to around 410,000 in 1624 after the Tokugawa Bakufu in Edo and the growing commerce of Osaka had drawn people away from the old capital.

The half million inhabitants of Hideyoshi's time are thought to have occupied as many as 180,000 houses. There is no map of the city extant from the Momoyama Period, and in fact the earliest existing map dates from the Kwanei Era (1624–44). Although the capital was almost entirely rebuilt by Hideyoshi, very few buildings erected by him exist today. A description of Momoyama Kyoto therefore depends largely upon literary sources. A Jesuit whom Father Cros cites as the Annalist of Macao recorded his impression of the capital nine years after its surrender to Nobunaga. "When we went to Japan in 1577," he wrote, "we found Kyoto very wretched. There were two quarters formed by a single street running north and south, with a few traverse lanes. The best houses, those of the *Kuge*, were of very poor exterior, and the *Kuge* themselves were indigent and poorly clad. What remained of the palace of the Shogun after the fire and sack of 1565 was protected only by an enclosure of earth and reeds, which had already fallen into ruin. The town properly so called formed a square with four immense suburbs." Thus the appearance of the city had evidently changed little since Xavier had seen it twenty-six years earlier.

When Nobunaga died in 1582, Kyoto for the most part still lay desolate as it had done since the Onin War more than a century before. All that remained of the old capital was a small section between First Avenue (Ichijo) and Fourth Avenue (Shijo) and from Takakura west to Horikawa, the street on which the present Nijo (Second Avenue) Castle was to be built early in the next century. In this area Nobunaga had erected a small palace for the Emperor and a mansion for the Shogun, but the latter had been burned when the Shogun was deposed in 1573. All around was open country, much of it uncultivated.

One of Hideyoshi's first appointments was Maeda Gen-i as the *Shoshidai*, or Governor of Kyoto. During 1585, the year Hideyoshi became kampaku, Maeda was entrusted with the duty of laying out a new capital with Hosokawa Fujitaka and Satamura Shokyu as his assistants. According to Father Frois, Hideyoshi in 1583 had considered moving the Emperor and the principal monasteries to Osaka but eventually had decided to retain Kyoto as the capital. Since experience had shown that the broad roads of the Heian capital had made street fighting easy, it was resolved to abolish the old forty-foot-wide streets and lay out new ones only twenty-one *shaku* (feet) in width, for despite the availability of Japanese-made matchlocks, much of the fighting was still done with swords and bows and arrows. The Heian plan of streets running parallel from north to south intersected at right angles by similar streets running east and west was kept, but the Heian Ukyo (Right Capital), empty for many centuries, was not rebuilt. Twenty-two main north-south streets and about fifty east-west streets were laid out under Maeda's direction. Covering about 3,500 acres, Hideyoshi's capital extended from Kuramaguchi on the north to Kujo (Ninth Avenue) on the south and from Teramachi on the east to Senbondori on the west. From Nijo southward the streets running east and west retained their old names; Teramachi today is the second street west of the Kamo River because in Hideyoshi's period the Odoi extended all along the banks paralleling the route of the present-day Kawaramachi. Beyond the Odoi was a large section of the city east of the Kamo with bridges at Sanjo, Shijo, and Gojo (Third, Fourth, and Fifth Avenues).

Employing forced labor suppplied by the feudal lords, the building of the Odoi was accomplished in less than five months in 1591. A moat sixty-five feet wide in some places ran along one or both sides, and guardhouses were located at each of the ten gates. The area enclosed was a huge oblong of about the same distance from north to south as present-day Kyoto. Within the Odoi the new city was divided into two sections. Everything north of Sanjo was known as Kami-Kyo (Upper Capital) and everything south as Shimo-Kyo (Lower Capital). Each section was given its own governor and officials who were subject to the *Shoshidai,* whose responsibility was the entire city. Almost all of the temples were rebuilt in two districts to the west and north and along Teramachi, which as the name indicates was the "street of temples." The imperial palace was erected in the same location east of Karasuma Street where it had been for several hundred years and still is today. A wide road appropriately named Gokomachi (Processional Street) was built from Fushimi to the palace gate in order that Hideyoshi might make a splendid progress from his castle to visit the Emperor. Hideyoshi chose the northeast corner of the old Daidairi, the site of the Heian imperial palace, to build his Jurakudai. Until this time the imperial enclosure, empty of buildings, had been a favorite hunting ground for the Kyoto noblemen. Around the Jurakudai were grouped the mansions of his officials. When Nijo Castle was commenced by Ieyasu in 1602, it was erected in the southeast corner of the imperial enclosure.

In Momoyama Kyoto, society contained four main classes. Highest in the social scale were the *kuge*, the hereditary aristocrats. Next came the *buke*, or warrior class including daimyo and samurai, and below them the *domin*, or peasants. The merchants and artisans (*chonin*) were fourth in rank. To the military government the social status of the *chonin* was lower than that of the samurai or the peasants, but official treatment of the *chonin* was vastly better than that of the peasant farmers. Lowest of all were the outcasts, the *hinin*. While the *kuge* no longer had any political power, they were much better off economically under Nobunaga and Hideyoshi than they had been for more than a century. Until the Momoyama Period, these descendants of the upper aristocracy were the only class that valued and preserved culture. They acted as conservators of the arts of literature, painting, and music and occupied themselves with performing the traditional court ceremonies. In earlier times they seldom married outside their class; now their blood was invigorated by marriage with samurai and even commoners.

Not until the period of Ieyasu did the *buke*, or *bushi* (warriors), become a fixed class. In the middle of the sixteenth century the demarcations between the samurai, the farmer, the artisan and the merchant were not strict. Until the end of the century almost any man of ability could carve out a career for himself. No age was so prolific in skillful generals, adventurous businessmen, and gifted artists. One explanation for this outpouring of talent may be the fact that the three military rulers were men of real genius who insisted that the promotion of subordinates should depend upon nothing but natural ability and devotion to duty. The *buke* in the time of Hideyoshi ranged in origin from upper aristocracy who had married samurai to peasants who had become retainers of warriors.

The Sengoku Jidai, the Age of the Country at War, was notable for the rise of peasants into the *buke* class. The greatest of these was Hideyoshi, but among others were Kato Kiyomasa, a peasant from Hideyoshi's own village who became a general in the Korean campaign; Okubo Nagayasu, a *sangaku* performer who developed Ieyasu's gold and silver mines; and Honda Masanobu, a falconer who carried out diplomatic missions for Ieyasu. The sixteenth century is often described as the golden age of the *bushi*, and modern writers like to think of it as a time when loyal fighting men were inspired to patriotic deeds by Bushido, the "way of the warrior." Actually it was an age of unscrupulous militarism when professional soldiers changed from one side to another depending upon how much money was offered. The military spirit was probably at its height in Nobunaga's time, for he was a popular and inspiring leader. Hideyoshi, less interested in the arts of war, was more concerned with imitating the manners and pursuits of the court nobility.

Understandably, the virtues most prized in the samurai were bravery and obedience. In earlier times they had been archers on horse or on foot, but the introduction of firearms, which made it easier to assemble armies of untrained farmers, tended to disintegrate the samurai class. This process continued until the surviving *bushi* were pressed into a rigidly defined group under the Tokugawa shogunate. The ordinary samurai had to maintain himself, his wife and family and their eight or ten servants out of an annual allowance of 150 or 200 *koku* of rice. While samurai traditionally were supposed to live simply and frugally, most of them had to do so out of necessity. It was not surprising that samurai found themselves in the clutches of moneylenders or attempted to escape their class and earn a living as tradesmen.

A law of 1585 declared that no person in service from a samurai down to a peasant farmer might leave his employment without permission of his overlord. In Kyoto, samurai were required to live near their lords and apart from the districts of shopkeepers and craftsmen. After Edo became the military capital, few samurai remained in Kyoto except for the garrisons at Nijo and Fushimi. All classes from noblemen to peasants were represented among the Buddhist and Shinto priests who were outside all social grades; abbots or other officials were usually from the *kuge* or *buke*. High government positions held by priests and priestly interference in politics have been mentioned previously. Several Buddhist sects permitted marriage, but Father Vilela, who stayed at Hieisan for a short time, and other European observers were shocked at the sodomy taking place openly in several of the Kyoto monasteries.

While millions of peasants still tilled the soil, other thousands escaped to the cities despite prohibitory laws. The most remarkable social change of the Momoyama Period was the rise of the common people brought about by the use of *ashigaru*, the foot soldiers who served the samurai, and by the increased commerce and industry which resulted from peace and the unification of the country. While a bold democratic spirit was pervading the nation, Hideyoshi was determined to keep the peasants on the land. After 1591 if any farmer abandoned his land and ran away to the city, his whole village was punished. Under Hideyoshi a lord could levy one man for compulsory labor for every field yielding 2,000 *koku* of rice. Paradoxically, it was by this means that so many thousands of peasants were torn from their homes and brought to Kyoto to work on Hideyoshi's vast building projects. Equally surprising is the fact that Hideyoshi, who had been born a peasant, did all in his power to prevent the rise of an independent class of tradesmen and artisans in Kyoto and other cities.

Just above the *eta*, the outcasts or "untouchables," were the *kojiki* who were beggars, necromancers, storytellers, dog trainers, acrobats, musicians, and actors. Lowest of the *kojiki* were the *joro*, or prostitutes, who made a precarious living on the streets. A girl from a desperately poor family might be sold into prostitution by her father, mother, or brothers, or she could be rented out for several months and then returned to her family. Many girls who later became perfectly respectable married women worked as prostitutes for a number of years to earn enough to buy clothes and household furnishings for their dowries. The *joro* haunted the area around the city gates where the road from Fushimi entered the capital. During the rule of Hideyoshi, daimyo and their retainers were required to stop at Fushimi before being admitted to the city. The many bawdyhouses on the road from Fushimi no doubt entertained them as they waited.

In striking contrast to the *joro* was the geisha, an accomplished singer, dancer, and musician, who was often so expensive only the wealthy could afford her company. Geisha had to serve a long apprenticeship as *maiko* (pupils) during which they learned reading, writing, and all the social graces which made them charming companions. Geisha houses, often very elaborately decorated, were concentrated by the seventeenth century on the east bank of the Kamo River around the Gion shrine, just across the river on the west bank, and in the Shimabara quarter northwest of the temple of Nishi Hongan-ji. During the Momoyama Period geisha frequently influenced fashions and manners. For example, when they began to pile their hair high on their heads, this innovation was generally adopted in Kyoto except by ladies of the court and *buke* who continued wearing their hair long and flowing.

Lowest of all the classes were the *eta*. They could eat meat, as strict Buddhists could not, they were compelled to marry other *eta*, and they could not reside outside their own community at the southeast edge of the city. Possibly the word "*eta*" came from *etori* (butcher) and not from two Chinese ideographs meaning "very dirty," from which in later times it was claimed to have been derived. The first *eta* had been set apart in Kyoto in the middle ages and included those who earned their living as butchers, dyers, cattle herders, fishermen, undertakers, tomb attendants, and midwives. Members of these occupations were considered defiled because they were involved in the taking of life, which was prohibited by Buddhism, or uncleanness, which was enjoined by Shintoism. The *eta* were forced to supply all of the public executioners, and a stigma was attached even to plasterers and makers of writing brushes and inks because their trades obliged them to handle the hair and bones of animals. Since the forbidden occupations included all the processes of making leather armor and sword belts for the samurai, some of the *eta* were very well off. *Eta* also made all of the *zori* (sandals) and *geta* (wooden clogs). In the Momoyama Period they seem not to have been feared or hated to the extent that they were later on, and until the seventeenth century perhaps some movement in or out of the class was possible.

The position of women in society had declined greatly since the tenth century when Lady Murasaki Shikibu had written the greatest of Heian novels, the *Genji Monogatari*. Respectable women no longer were treated as the intellectual equals of men. Women of the nobility were strictly secluded and seldom went out of the mansion enclosure. Middle-class women had more freedom, and most shop clerks and many street hawkers were women. Wives were regarded as little better than household servants who performed specialized duties.

All three of the military rulers transferred daimyo from one part of the country to another for political reasons. When the daimyo were moved, all the samurai had to follow their lord to his new fief or into exile as the case might be. Since every samurai was compelled to be married, the men divorced their first wives and remarried in the new locality. When daimyo exchanged fiefs, samurai frequently exchanged wives. Hideyoshi tried to prevent the samurai from keeping concubines because of the dissension caused by illegitimate children. When this attempt was not successful, he declared two concubines to be the maximum. Any man could have concubines if he could afford them, yet his wife must remain completely virtuous. She was obliged to cater to every whim of her husband and to be diligent in her household tasks, for custom allowed him to divorce his wife without an explanation, or even to kill her if he chose. Mothers were accorded the highest respect by their sons, it is true, and the influence of a mother on her son was often very great, but the young wife who was brought to live in the home of her mother-in-law was likely to be treated with extreme harshness by all members of the family and particularly by her husband's mother. Women, children, and servants were all subject to the head of the household and could be killed on the spot for the slightest disobedience.

A father selected as heir his most promising son, who was not necessarily the eldest. In business or the arts, the adoption of a boy from outside the family was common if a man was childless or if none of his children was sufficiently talented. Early retirement, practiced by all classes from the emperor himself to merchants and artisans, had the advantage of freeing a man from responsibility yet allowing him at the same time to keep control of his affairs. Children of all classes were well behaved and were rarely disciplined with blows. The missionaries noticed that children were never heard using crude language or seen fighting with one another and that even seven- or eight-year-olds acted with "such incredible gravity and maturity" that they seemed more like adults than children.

The missionaries were agreed that the Japanese people were the politest they had ever met. They were "courteous above measure," declared Will Adams, an English pilot who had arrived in Japan in 1600. "Even the common folk and peasants are well brought up and so remarkably polite that they give the impression they were trained at court," wrote Father Valignano. All classes were taught good manners; the maid serving tea moved in a style similar to that used at court ceremonials, and shop clerks were taught to sit and stand in patterns like those in the No plays. Everywhere in Japan a Kyoto accent, because of its long association with the court and literature, was considered the indication of a cultivated person.

Valignano related that even when two men were deadly enemies, they would both smile at each other and never fail to perform the customary courtesies. "They are the most affable people," continued Valignano, "and a race given to outward marks of affection than any yet known. They have such control over their anger and impatience that it is almost a miracle to witness any quarrel or insulting words whether with one another or with foreigners." But foreigners in Japan were disturbed by what seemed to them evidence of Japanese duplicity and treachery. The usual opinion about this trait was reflected by Father Rodrigues when he wrote, "It is said that they have three hearts: a false one in their mouths for all the world to see, another in their breasts only for their friends, and the third in the depths of their hearts, reserved for themselves alone and never manifested to anybody." From childhood they were taught never to reveal their feelings and always to appear outwardly calm. From this reluctance to expose themselves to deception or embarrassment came the custom of conducting business of a delicate nature through a third party. Even fathers and sons never discussed anything serious with each other but only through a third person. Members of the same household often dealt with one another by sending servants with written messages.

Besides this never failing politeness, patience, and seemingly unemotional acceptance of discomfort and hardships, foreign visitors were aware of other qualities in the citizens of Kyoto. Among these was a reverence for ancestors, for Buddhist and Shinto deities, and for the emperor; temples and shrines were thronged with worshipers every day. Their easygoing gaiety was expressed in the frequent festivals for which the capital was renowned, their love of nature in the tiny gardens hidden within every house, in picnics to view cherry blossoms or maple leaves, or in pilgrimages to the top of Hieisan. The militarism and patriotism for which the samurai were celebrated were characteristics to be found in every class. The Japanese were the "most warlike and bellicose race yet discovered on the earth," asserted Valignano in 1580.

Finally, the one quality which distinguished the common people above all else from their counterparts in sixteenth century Europe was cleanliness. Every western visitor mentioned it. Not only were the streets clean and the houses immaculate, but even the lower classes bathed at least once a day. Coming from Renaissance Europe where a bath was conventionally considered a definite health hazard, the missionaries were dubious about the value of washing oneself so frequently and were scandalized to discover that both sexes bathed together in the public bathhouses. When the Japanese in turn considered the characteristics of the Portuguese traders, they found them greedy, quarrelsome, uncultured adventurers whose rough manners lacked the courtesies which were so scrupulously observed by all classes in Japan. They were somewhat more impressed by the aesthetic tastes and scientific knowledge of the missionaries.

To govern the people of the capital, Nobunaga in the autumn of 1574 established the office of *Shoshidai*, a title retained from the Ashikaga Bakufu. Murai Sadakatsu, who had been in charge of building the imperial palace, was appointed and opened a bureau for his staff near the corner of Sanjo and Kyogoku. From this location of the *Shoshidai*'s office all distances in the empire were calculated. Soon after Hideyoshi was settled in the capital, he appointed five *Bugyo* as commissioners to govern the city and the Gokinai. Maeda Gen-i, who had been a priest at Hieisan and had a good literary background, was made *Shoshidai* with further duties concerning religious matters and as a judge in civil suits. Natsuka Masaie was put in charge of public finance, the reforming of taxes and weights, and the coining of gold. As a representative of the Toyotomi family, Hideyoshi chose Asano Nagamasa, whose wife was the younger sister of Yodogimi, Hideyoshi's favorite mistress. The Governor of Lower Kyoto and chief of police was Ishida Mitsunari. The fifth *Bugyo* was Mashida Nagamori who was made commissioner for public works and supervisor of taxation and finance.

After the battle of Sekigahara (1600), Maeda Gen-i retired to his domain in Tamba, having served as *Shoshidai* for seventeen years. Following two temporary appointments, Ieyasu made Itakura Katsushige the *Shoshidai* in September, 1601. Itakura resided with his family just north of Nijo Castle, which was placed in his charge. His duties were to maintain order in the city with the aid of fifty *Yoriki* (police) and one hundred *Doshin* (constables), to administer justice in the thirteen western provinces, and to keep a close watch on the activities of the court, restraining the imperial family and *kuge* from any interference in the administration of the country. To prevent imperial correspondence with enemies of the Tokugawa, Itakura was responsible for the dispatch of messengers from Kyoto to other parts of the empire and for the reception in the capital of envoys to the imperial court. As he was the direct officer of the Shogun in Kyoto, he had to be a Fudai daimyo, a relative of the Tokugawa family. In name all the old court officials were retained, and Ieyasu himself took the position of *udaijin*, the third highest rank at court, but the emperor and his nobles had no political authority and were urged to devote all their attention to poetry, music, and the fine arts.

Neither Nobunaga nor Hideyoshi developed a comprehensive system of law, and neither seems to have had much interest in legal principles. Consequently, the ordinary citizen had little contact with representatives of the military government. Before the arrival of Nobunaga the *za* under the direction of well-to-do merchants had managed the affairs of each street. This arrangement was practical inasmuch as people living next to each other were usually engaged in the same trade. A similar scheme was continued by Hideyoshi and the Tokugawa. At the junction of every two streets were four gates, each one closing the entrance of a street. When these wooden gates were shut at night, nobody could go out without a pass which had to be presented to the chief officer of the street. This chief officer, who was chosen by the inhabitants, was known as the *kumi-no-oya* ("father of the group"). In addition, each street had a secretary who checked passports and kept registers of births, deaths, and marriages; a treasurer; and a messenger who announced proclamations from the *Shoshidai* and other city officials.

The inhabitants of the street were divided into five-man groups (*gonin-gumi*) who were responsible for each other. If one member committed a crime, the others were punished as well. Neighbors were obliged to stop quarrels or be held accountable. The *kumi-no-oya* had to know every person who came to live in his street, for he could be made to suffer for any unlawful act on his block. Under this stern system of collective responsibility, the head of the family could be punished for the crimes of his servants or lodgers, children for crimes of their parents, and corporations for individual members. The *kumi-no-oya* also had the responsibility of selecting householders for the night watch, giving orders in the event of fire, and keeping buckets, a fire hook, and a ladder ready near his home. Householders were sometimes punished when they were unable to stop the spread of a fire into another street, for it was the duty of everyone to prevent accidents from occurring.

The one feature of Japanese law which astonished Europeans most frequently was this custom of punishing not only the criminal but also his relatives and neighbors. Everybody had fixed obligations and duties and risked punishment for not performing them properly, but in Japanese law the idea that the common man had any rights was inconceivable. The chief officer of the street settled all small crimes, both civil and criminal, and ordered punishments. If a crime was too serious or too complicated to be ruled upon by the street magistrate, it was taken to the governor. Hideyoshi is reported to have erected the first prison in Kyoto composed of several huts where the prisoners were kept under guard. A large prison was unnecessary, since death or banishment was the punishment for serious offenses. Condemned members of the aristocracy were allowed to commit *harakiri* (in Chinese, *seppuku*); common criminals were beheaded or crucified. European travelers professed to be horrified at seeing severed heads lining the Sanjo bridge or decaying corpses hanging from crosses near the Fushimi gate, but on the whole, Japanese executions were no more barbarous than European ones of the same period.

All the costs of governing the capital and of such civic improvements as streets, canals, and bridges were in theory borne by the military rulers. In practice, work on building projects was done by the citizens or by laborers conscripted by the daimyo. It was true that no land or property taxes were levied on residents. Formerly a tax called the *Jishi-sen* had been assessed by the Ashikaga shogunate on all inhabitants of the city who owned houses or land. Nobunaga not only exempted Kyoto from the *Jishi-sen* tax but lent money to the citizens to encourage trade and industry. Tenants who were renting were exempt from taxation, as was the land belonging to court nobles or temples. Wine dealers, pawnbrokers, and storekeepers paid licensing taxes. Nobunaga did not attempt to collect taxes from the daimyo but relied upon gifts of gold and silver at New Year's. The daimyo competed with each other in presenting money and splendid gifts to Hideyoshi and Ieyasu, both of whom continued to exempt Kyoto from taxation.

While Kyoto was enriched by Hideyoshi's tremendous building projects and his ostentatious entertainments, he did not pay for any of these himself. Labor, materials, and the rice to feed the thousands of workmen were all requisitioned from the feudal lords. As Kyoto, Osaka, Fushimi, and Sakai were all in Hideyoshi's possession, a sizable part of the wealth brought to these cities by merchants and daimyo found its way into Hideyoshi's treasury through sales taxes and import duties. Sections of rice land in the vicinity of the city were allotted to the imperial court to provide an income.

Hideyoshi felt that respect for the court was good policy and helped to stabilize the country, but unfortunately for the court, the allotted land was more or less exhausted by centuries of cultivation and neglect during the wars. Ieyasu continued to base the imperial revenue on this land, no doubt with the expectation that the Emperor would never be able to live in an extravagant fashion.The Tokugawa shoguns depended for their income on control of thousands of acres of rice lands and ownership of almost all the country's gold and silver mines. The freedom from land and property taxes of the Kyoto citizen was typical of his relationship with the shogunate. If, on the one hand, he had little share in determining how he was to be governed, on the other, interference with his daily life by the military government was, in most circumstances, minimal.

Because of the presence of the imperial court and the great temples and shrines, large numbers of craftsmen producing luxury articles had worked in Kyoto ever since its founding. Throughout the centuries they had been stimulated by the styles and techniques of paintings, sculptures, textiles, and other beautiful objects imported by the aristocracy from China and the Asian continent. Swordsmiths, makers of lacquer ware, or weavers of silken brocades could devote countless hours of meticulous handwork to attain levels of craftsmanship possible only with the bountiful patronage of the emperors and shoguns. When the power of the imperial court and the shogunate passed into the hands of the military rulers, these craftsmen had been established for such a long time that Kyoto continued as the center for the production of luxury articles. Hideyoshi, in particular, loved to dress in gorgeous costumes and surrounded himself with opulent furnishings. Even after the military capital was moved to Edo during the administration to the parsimonious Ieyasu, the rich provincial daimyo visited the old capital to purchase the newest fashions in clothes or ceramics.

Along with removing such limitations on trade as the toll barriers, Nobunaga had abolished the *za*, the trade guilds which for several hundred years had monopolized manufacturing processes and retail trade. In spite of the greater freedom enjoyed by tradesmen after the abolition of the *za*, the manufacture of many products could not be carried on without the association of various kinds of workers. The creation of a religious statue, for instance, might require the services of wood carvers, metalworkers, and lacquer painters. Collectively these artisans were called *shokunin*. Because of this necessity for close relationships between the *shokunin*, new guilds were founded in place of the *za*, mutually respecting the ties between artisans and merchants. These guilds customarily had a ten-year apprenticeship period for young boys and girls during which they learned a trade while living in the house of the master. This period was followed by a year or two of courtesy service.

One of Hideyoshi's first acts after the death of Nobunaga was to urge all the weavers who had settled in Sakai during the civil wars to return to Kyoto. In the northwestern part of the city a special quarter for weavers named Nishijin (Western Camp) had been developed about 1570. Chinese weavers escaping from Ming China were brought to Nishijin, and with them came various weaving secrets, especially a much sought after method of making gold thread. Even though sumptuary laws limited the wearing of silk clothing to the priests and the aristocracy, the rising merchant class wore kimonos with hidden linings of metallic brocade. By the seventeenth century there were more than five thousand looms, and the weavers of Nishijin all but monopolized the weaving of silk fabrics used by the court, the shoguns, the daimyo, the temples, the monasteries, and the No actors. The city was also a center for the production of cotton cloth which, like weaving, was concentrated in a special district. As the dyes were fixed by washing the cotton in the clear waters of the Kamo, much of the manufacturing took place in a section to the northeast of the Sanjo bridge. The great concentration of dyers in this district did not occur until the end of the seventeenth century, however, when so-called Yuzen dyeing was invented.

Some type of handicraft was carried on in very nearly every house in the city. All the members of one trade lived side by side in certain streets. Apothecaries and brewers could be found on Nijo along with storehouses for sake, soy sauce, and bean paste. Several streets were lined with warehouses for the large quantities of luxury goods imported from China, East Asia, and Europe. Storehouses were constructed for protecting possessions placed in pawn, the pawnbrokers thus becoming warehousemen as well as moneylenders. There were whole streets of carpenters, *geta*-makers, blacksmiths, silversmiths, and gold brokers. The most important east-west road for shopping was Sanjo, the Kyoto end of the Tokaido, which extended 310 miles through the Pacific coast provinces to Edo. At Awataguchi, where the Tokaido entered the city through the eastern mountains, were kilns for baking pottery; just east of the Sanjo bridge lived the makers of bronze mirrors; and westward beyond the many inns around the bridge were needle and fan shops. Farther along Sanjo metal bathtubs and temple bells were cast. West of the Kamo on Gojo were the houses of dollmakers, poem-card writers and tinworkers.

In the seventeenth century on Kyogoku just west of the Odoi were shops selling horn and antler products, leather goods, Buddhist prayer beads, and musical instruments such as *samisen* and *koto*. On Gokomachi were carvers of religious statues, paper-toy makers, and jade sculptors; on Muromachi shops offered pongee, thread, hemp kimonos, and silk *kosode*. On Nishinotoin madder and tannin dyers were grouped. Farther west on Omiya were sellers of lumber, bamboo poles, charcoal, Tamba tobacco, and cedar bark. In hot summer days the narrow streets between Sanjo and Nijo could be covered by drawing canvas blinds across from one side to the other. Other streets had arcades under which passers-by could walk to avoid the rain or sun. Hanging from these arcades in front of the shops were bamboo curtains to protect the goods from dust, and each shop had a curtain in front of its door painted with an animal, number, or symbol to serve as a name or identification. Artisans who had been attracted to Fushimi to work on the castle continued to reside there, making it a center for painters and wood carvers. Many brewers of sake moved in because the quality of Fushimi water was so good, and the Yodo River provided a convenient means of transportation. Soon the road between the castle and Kyoto was lined with houses, shops, and inns, extending the built-up area of the city several miles to the south.

In Heian times trade and industry were not clearly distinguished, but in the late sixteenth century there was more of a distinction between merchants and artisans. Indeed, merchants trading with foreign countries were prohibited from engaging in industry. In 1593 Hideyoshi instituted a system of ships licensed under the August Red Seal. These armed merchantmen, which traded all over the eastern Pacific as far as Siam, belonged to such Kyoto merchant-venturer families as the Chaya and Sumikura. In these Kyoto-owned ships were exported Japanese lacquer work, screens, fans, umbrellas, swords, paper, copper, and camphor. Among the imports were cotton, wool, silk, sugar, incense, and drugs. The Yodo River was the chief means of communication between the capital and the ports of Sakai and Osaka on the Inland Sea. Although the capital was not a seaport, it was the chief mercantile city of Japan in the early seventeenth century.

Whereas trade both at home and abroad had previously been carried on by barter, a money economy became feasible in the final decades of the sixteenth century. Copper coins, mostly from China, had been in circulation in Kyoto before Nobunaga's occupation in 1568. The following year he issued a proclamation requiring that articles for sale be priced only in gold and silver coins. The stocks of gold and silver bullion accumulated by the mining activities of the daimyo had made this coinage possible, but the demand for gold was so great much had to be imported from the continent. After about 1585 Hideyoshi employed a Kyoto family of metal workers named Goto to mint coins known as *Tensho* from the Tensho Era (1573–91). Between 1601 and 1695 gold and silver coins minted in Kyoto were called *Keicho*, again from the era name. As the coins were not always the same weight, merchants who were buying and selling carried scales. There was such a spurt of exchange activity during the last half of the century that the value of money remained about the same, even though the volume in circulation was much greater. Fortunately, the large number of coins being minted did not lead to an inflationary rise in prices.

The palace of the emperor, the mansion of the wealthy merchant, and the house of the artisan differed in number of rooms and costliness of materials, but the architectural arrangement, household articles, and method of heating and cooking all had the same basic forms, shapes, sizes, and functions. In fact, the wealthy merchant and the poor artisan often lived side by side on the same narrow street, and from the outside it was impossible to guess that behind the weathered wooden door of the merchant's house were rooms with jade statues, precious ceramics, and golden screens. Tradition and convention were far stronger factors in shaping Japanese architecture than was the climate. Houses in the capital were designed to meet the requirements of the four hot, damp months of summer and not the bitter cold of January and February. The open plan provided cross ventilation during muggy weather, and the wide roof overhang protected the open rooms from the rain, but it was a type of dwelling utterly unsuited to Kyoto's weather for half the year.

Japanese civilization was the only major one never to have created furniture. Because everyone sat and slept on the floor, the removal of shoes before entering the house was an absolute necessity. As there was no furniture, rooms could be small with the entire living area opened up by shoving aside movable screens. After the triumph of the Tokugawa Bakufu, the size of a house was fixed by law according to the rank of the owner. In the second half of the sixteenth century, floors in upper-class homes were completely covered with the mats called *tatami*, made of pressed rice straw overlaid with rushes woven in a design of narrow parallel stripes and the edges bound in black tape. In Kyoto a standard *tatami* size of 6.30 inches long by 3.15 inches wide and 2.12 inches thick was established, the number of mats determining the size of the rooms. Standard measurements for the posts and beams which framed the house were based on these *tatami* sizes.

Houses were constructed with wooden frames supporting the heavy protective roof. By bringing precut lumber to the site it was possible to erect a house in two days. The aristocracy used cedar (*sugi*) or cypress (*hinoki*), and commoners built of pine (*matsu*). To begin, upright posts were placed on stones to prevent the wood from touching the earth. Transverse beams (*nageshi*) were then mortised into these posts. Between the frames the spaces were filled with walls of mud applied to a lath of bamboo and then covered with about one-sixteenth of an inch of plaster. Because the walls had no structural function other than to support themselves, openings could be placed at any point, and rooms could be freely arranged within this framework of posts and beams. An entire house built in this way could be taken apart and moved to another place. Before the sixteenth century outside openings had been closed with wooden shutters which could be pulled up out of the way, but in Momoyama houses sliding doors covered with translucent paper came into general use. Called *shoji* ("interceptor"), they slid in tracks on the under side of the *nageshi*. The solid inside sliding doors which separated the interior into rooms were named *fusuma* ("bed quilt") because originally the pattern of the thick paper which covered both sides looked like a bed quilt.

Most Kyoto houses were only one story in height, although some prosperous merchants had homes with a low second floor. Roofs were covered with bark fastened down by strips of wood. Occasionally they were thatched with straw or reeds, but this type was more commonly found in the country. As straw or bark roofs were so easily set on fire, edicts were issued in the seventeenth century requiring all town houses to be built with tiled roofs. In the homes of the poor, rooms were open to the rafters, but the more prosperous built ceilings of thin boards, overlapping at the edges and laid on narrow beams. Through the cracks dust was showered down on the faces of people sleeping below by rats scurrying about at night. Large residences had solid coffered ceilings decorated with lacquer and paintings. Ceilings were called *tenjo* ("well of heaven") because the squares in the coffered type were the shape of the Chinese ideogram for "well."

The buildings of aristocratic mansions were set back from the street and surrounded with a high wall entered by a roofed gateway. Some merchants had Chinese style residences with the rooms arranged around a paved center courtyard and blank walls on the street, but in the typical Kyoto house, the room on the street side was a shop (*mise*) in which products were both fabricated and sold. Shutters on the street side could be lifted up or slid aside to open a raised area covered with *tatami* on which the shopkeeper and his assistants sat and on which were set out examples of his goods. The customers stood at the edge of the street. Behind this shop was the house in which the master, his family, and his assistants lived. The private rooms were separated from the shop by the *niwa*, a tiny courtyard garden. On the other side of this garden was a kitchen with a dirt floor. The sliding doors in the kitchen, called *koshi-taka shoji*, were papered only on their upper half, the lower being solid wood.

The chief feature of the kitchen was a stove built up of clay plastered over and containing one large or as many as seven smaller fireplaces, each with a hole on top on which a kettle could be placed. The stove was an important object regarded with deep veneration, and less sophisticated people still worshiped a kitchen deity as they had in archaic times. At this period the arrangement of the kitchen was influenced by the *mizu-ya*, or tea kitchen used in the tea ceremony, and every utensil had its exact place to conform with rules for movement. The cupboards, latticed with bamboo so that breezes but not flies could enter, had their legs mounted in stone basins to keep out ants.

Beyond the kitchen was the living room which in the Momoyama Period was likely to have in one wall a *tokonoma* and in another the cupboards for clothing and bedding. Merchants kept their valuable goods locked away in the *kura*, a detached stone fireproof room, the only example of a masonry building to be found in domestic architecture. The living room was warmed by a *kotatsu*, a sunken grate with its top level with the *tatami*. Over the top of the grate in the winter was placed a square table covered with a quilt under which the whole family sat to warm themselves. *Byobu*, low screens made of several thicknesses of paper pasted on both sides of a wooden framework, were arranged to keep drafts from people seated on the *tatami*. While larger homes had a bathroom with a sunken wooden tub, common people had to go to the public baths.

Concealed at the end of an outside corridor of the house was the privy, or *kawa-ya* (literally, "river-house"), perhaps so named because the first were built over streams. In ordinary homes it was an oblong slot in the floor with a large jar underneath which was cleaned out through an opening in the wall beside it. The contents were purchased with money or rice by farmers to fertilize their rice fields. Elegant residences had compartments in the garden called *Daibenjo* (Great Convenience Place) which were built of beautiful woods, decorated with paintings, and surrounded by miniature rock gardens. Some tea houses had two privies, one, the *kafuku setsuin*, intended for use, the other *kazari setsuin*, strictly for show. Both were duly inspected by the guests before the tea ceremony to see if Zen standards of cleanliness had been observed and also to make sure no enemies were lurking there. Daimyo had *Daibenjo* as large as six mats to provide plenty of room to maneuver with a sword if attacked. The privy was cleaned out by the attendant and new paper cut after each guest had departed. Each time, a ewer of fresh water was supplied, for, as Father Rodrigues found to his astonishment, it was "an invariable custom of both nobles and commoners to wash their hands every time after use." The beauty, neatness, and charm of

Kyoto's houses were constantly praised by the Jesuit fathers. "Judging from the experience of Father Gaspar Vilela, Brother Luis de Almeida, and myself," wrote Father Frois, "it is my opinion that nobody can see them for the first time without feeling within himself great admiration."

The custom of sitting on the floor made loose garments the most comfortable and the most practical. In the Momoyama Period there was a general simplification of clothing. Because the miseries of the civil wars had forced the aristocracy to modify the elaborate costumes of former times, nobles and commoners alike began to wear simple, short kimonos called *kosode* which had originated with the lower classes. For court ceremonies the exaggerated styles of the Heian Era were still worn. Court ladies dressed themselves in five different colored robes with a long train over a *kosode*, under which were full, baggy trousers, the *hakama*. Noblemen wore a costume consisting of a short jacket with a train from four to twelve feet or more in length depending on rank, wide *hakama*, and over these, two large, square-cut, double-breasted robes. The shape of court hats, which were made of black silk gauze, indicated the wearer's rank. Hats were not normally worn in the street by *kuge*, but for picnics in the country noblemen might wear a low crowned hat with a broad brim, and ladies a hat like an inverted bowl from which hung a white curtain three to four feet long.

Samurai usually dressed in a full, square-cut coat (*hitatare*) of silk or hemp with sleeves slashed at the shoulders so they could be dropped for fighting. The narrow sleeved *hitatare* worn under armor was made of expensive brocade, figured silk or tie-dyed material. Like the nobles, samurai wore wide *hakama*. From the age of thirteen *buke* were allowed to carry a sword (*katana*) and a dagger (*waki-*

zashi). Samurai are said to have inaugurated the practice of shaving the front and crown of the head with a razor, because of the weight of the helmet. Their long hair was drawn back from the middle of the skull downward toward the nape of the neck, neatly tied, and brought forward over the shaved crown in a top knot. This style came into vogue for civilians as well as soldiers. Youngsters let their forelock grow very long and tossed it back over the shaved part. A fastidious samurai perfumed his hair and helmet with incense and oil before going into battle in order that he might not be considered lacking in refinement should he be defeated and his head carried away. Beards and mustaches were esteemed by the warriors. Men and women of the *kuge* and *buke* classes, except young girls and widows, blackened their teeth. This custom, a disturbing one to European observers, was not followed by the lower classes. Among Hideyoshi's regulations of 1586 were restrictions on the style and materials of dress for the various grades of samurai. These prohibitions against the use of brocade and other rich materials, which were intended to preserve the simplicity and hardihood of the *buke* class, were enforced in Kyoto but not in the provinces.

Streetwear for men and women of the merchant and artisan classes consisted of a *kosode* tied with a belt (*obi*), and over it a three-quarter-length kimono, the *haori*. Under the *kosode*, women wore one or more petticoats or underskirts and men a cotton loin cloth. *Kosode* were lined with heavy padding for winter or with a thin lining (*awase*) for spring and autumn. Summer *kosode*, called *katabira*, had no lining and were often transparent. In the Momoyama Period only narrow *obi* were worn, but they were often beautifully embroidered or woven of silk in plaid or check patterns. According to a popular tale, courtesans who were entertaining the soldiers in Kyushu during the Korean campaign wore a knotted cord wound three or four times around the waist and tied with the long ends in front. This style was soon copied by all the women in Kyoto except the court ladies who continued to wear a ribbonlike *obi* of black and gold brocade. For dress occasions men wore the *kami-shimo* ("upper-lower"), vertically plaited *hakama*, into which was tucked a kind of jumper with winglike shoulders. Women are shown in Momoyama drawings wearing the *koshimaki* ("wrapped around the waist"), an outer kimono which was tied on with the shoulders and sleeves hanging below the waist.

Peasant men dressed in a white cotton loincloth, blue cotton leggings, straw sandals, a dark blue cotton apron over the chest, and a short dark blue coat. The missionaries were offended at seeing pike bearers, chair carriers, and farmers who had tucked up their coats above their waists leaving nothing but a narrow girdle of cloth about their loins. European visitors noted that many workmen had tattooed legs. Peasant women wore a square of cotton cloth folded around the hips, a short petticoat, and at least one full-length kimono under a blue *kosode*. In the hot summer they often discarded some of their upper garments and, tying up their skirts round their waists, exposed considerably more than Europeans were accustomed to seeing. Familiar figures on Kyoto streets were the Buddhist priests clothed in a white kimono with a shawl-like hood and over it a *koromo*, a black robe of hemp with sleeves so wide and long they reached almost to the ground. All classes wore sandals (*zori*) with a sole of twisted straw, rope, or leather. Sandals were left at the outside door, and in cold weather *tabi* (bifurcated socks) were slipped on for walking on the *tatami*. *Geta* (wooden clogs), kept in place by a thong between the first two toes, were practical wear for muddy streets. Some *geta* illustrated in paintings of the period were at least six inches tall.

The adoption of the *kosode* by both sexes and all classes, including the military rulers themselves, was indicative of the new freedom which common people enjoyed at this time. As the cut of the *kosode* was so simple, all the attention was lavished on materials of beautiful design and texture. The splendor of the period found expression in boldly patterned textiles which were hardly rivaled anywhere in the world and never surpassed in Japan. Stimulated by woven and dyed textiles from Ming China and figured or striped weaves brought by the Portuguese from the South Seas, the Near East, and Europe, the Nishijin weavers soon learned to imitate all of these *meibutsu-kire* ("celebrated textiles"). The secret of making gold thread by pasting gold leaf to paper and twisting it around thin strips of silk was brought from China to Kyoto in the Tensho Era (1573–91), and from then on glittering *karaori* fabrics designed to imitate embroidery by means of weaving were produced in Nishijin. Although the name signifies "Chinese weaving," it was really a Japanese invention by a Nishijin weaver, Tawaraya. The outer robes worn by No actors in female roles are still called *karaori*. Shortly after 1500 a very complicated method of decorating cloth was introduced. Called *tsuji-ga-hana* ("flowers in crisscross") the designs were made by stitched tie-dyeing, then outlined with black ink and retouched in color. The technique which developed most remarkably was not dyeing but embroidery. Most typical of the period was the textile called *nuihaku* in which the pattern was a combination of gold foil and amazingly fine embroidery. Rich brocades were further embellished by pressing gold dust or gold leaf onto designs drawn in wet paste. The most astonishing Momoyama *kosode* were called *katami-gawari* ("two sides differing") made of two contrasting materials in bold, unexpected colors and patterns. A typical example showed, on the left side, purple clematis blossoms on black and gold *nuihaku*, and on the right, a red material patterned in folding fans and pampas grass. Hideyoshi owned a cloak of silk which had arrow and paulownia designs on a green background and sections around the shoulders and below the knees dyed purple. If a man did not have a fan in his sash, it was a true sign of poverty. Even priests carried them and, when they preached, emphasized their points by striking the table in front of them with a closed fan. The frames were usually made of white-cypress wood tied together with silk cords, and fan papers were often decorated by the greatest painters. Both men and woman carried oiled paper umbrellas as a protection against the sun and the almost daily rains. Straw raincoats and straw rain skirts worn by country people were a common sight in Kyoto streets.

After the appearance of Portuguese sailors and merchants in the city, a mania for foreign dress and foreign manners seized the capital. According to Frois, Nobunaga in 1569 had a great variety of Portuguese costumes including "scarlet capes, velvet caps with their feathers, and medallions of Our Lady of Grace." That even Hideyoshi followed this fashionable craze is evident from Father Pasio's often quoted letter of September, 1594. The Kampaku, he wrote, "has become so enamored of Portuguese dress and costume that he and his retainers frequently wear this apparel as do all the lords of Japan . . . with rosaries of driftwood on the breast above all their clothing, and with a crucifix at their side, or hanging from the waist, and sometimes even with kerchiefs in their hands; some of them are so curious that they learn by rote the litanies of *Pater Noster* and *Ave Maria* and go along praying in the streets, not in mockery or scorn of the Christians, but simply for gallantry."

Pipes were as fashionable as crucifixes for decorating costumes. Tobacco was imported by the Portuguese near the end of the century, and the first tobacco fields were planted just west of Kyoto a few years later. It became the mode to wear very long pipes with an attached pouch stuck through the sash. Hideyoshi is said to have prohibited smoking, and Ieyasu issued a decree against it in 1612, doubtless because it was contrary to his principles of economy. But even the Tokugawa Bakufu could not suppress smoking, and in the seventeenth century officials made few attempts to enforce the severe penalties. Exemplifying this extreme interest in everything foreign were the large numbers of so-called *Namban byobu* or "Southern Barbarian screens" painted in Kyoto. These often illustrated the arrival of a Portuguese ship and the disembarkation of fidalgos richly dressed in scarlet and gold, followed by Negro slaves and coolies bearing exotic gifts and leading Arabian horses and Bengal tigers.

Rich and poor ate the same foods, prepared to a very few standard recipes. The wealthy consumed larger quantities and had somewhat more variety, but the basic food for everyone was rice with a few fruits and vegetables and a little fish. Around Kyoto the greater part of the land consisted of irrigated rice fields where a second crop of wheat, barley, soya beans, sesame, and such vegetables as cucumbers, turnips, and *daikon* (huge radishes) was raised in spring and autumn. Oranges and lemons came from Kii Province south of Kyoto; grapes were raised in Kai near Fujisan. Melons, pears, peaches, apricots, plums, cherries, and other fruits were eaten fresh or pickled and preserved in vinegar and sugar. Europeans observing pomegranates, mangoes, and artichokes in Kyoto shops commented on the semitropical climate of the region.

All kinds of fish, especially carp from Omi Province and salt fish from Echigo on the Sea of Japan, were plentiful and inexpensive. To the dismay of Europeans, fish was frequently served raw (*sashimi*). Ducks, geese, and chickens were sold in the city by farmers, and hunters brought in pheasants, quail, doves, and partridges. Captain John Saris of the English East India Company noticed an abundance of pigs, goats, and sheep, but it was an unusual occasion when common people could afford meat of any kind, and in any case many Buddhists observed the injunctions against eating the flesh of four-footed animals. As the Gokinai was a center of cotton raising, large presses in the city furnished cottonseed oil for cooking. The customary drink for everyone was tea, which had been grown around Uji, just south of the capital, since the thirteenth century.

People ate only twice a day, the usual meal consisting of boiled rice (*meshi*) varied with noodles, bean cakes, vegetables, or seaweed, depending upon the affluence of the family. In poorer homes it was eaten from a common dish with everyone dipping into the bowl with the two small sticks called *hashi*. In well-to-do families each person had his own red or black lacquer table on which was set a nest of four lacquer bowls (*ireko*). Into the largest was placed the hot rice which was covered by the third vessel. The second customarily contained soup and the smallest a vegetable or fish. Everything was brought to the table cut up in small pieces and arranged with attention to color and texture. Foreigners found this food pleasing to look at but not to eat. Tea and sake, hot rice wine, were served in ceramic bowls. Elaborate pronouncements on the etiquette of eating and drinking and the arts of cooking were issued during the time of Hideyoshi, and ladies of the upper classes even employed a different vocabulary in naming dishes than men did.

4

Shinto, Buddhism, and Kirishitan

THE JESUIT MISSIONARIES soon discovered that the perplexing array of gods worshiped in thousands of Kyoto shrines actually belonged to two different religions. Buddhism they had previously encountered in India and Ceylon, but the indigenous Japanese cult of Shintoism was new to them. In the sixteenth century, Shinto, the Way of the Gods, was overshadowed both politically and culturally by the power of the Buddhists. Diverse in its origins, Shinto embraced archaic fertility cults together with the worship of nature, ancestors, and heroes. Amaterasu, the sun goddess, for example, was the chief deity not only of nature worshipers but of ancestor worshipers as well. Shinto shrines were built to protect an object which could be inhabited by a spirit, the *kami*. This word usually translated as "god" literally means "upper," as in Kami-kyo (Upper Capital). Rocks, trees, mountains, streams, anything that evoked awe or mystery, could contain a *kami*. Originating as fertility rites, the principal Shinto ceremonies were intended as services of purification.

The priests of all except the most important shrines were ordinary persons who combined some regular occupation with their priestly duties. To Shinto in the sixth century had been added Buddhism, introduced from Korea. Soon after the founding of Kyoto, Saicho, the builder of the Tendai monastery on Hieisan, announced that Shinto was in reality a primitive form of Buddhism and that Shinto deities were simply so many incarnations of Buddha. These ideas were reiterated by Saicho's rival and contemporary, Kukai, the founder of Shingon Buddhism. Buddhist priests began to take part in Shinto rites, and from the ninth century Buddhists promoted the fusion of the two religions. To a considerable extent, Shinto owed its survival into the sixteenth century to the circumstance that this fusion had occurred and that most of its shrines were controlled by powerful Buddhist sects. In view of the prevalent political conditions, Hachiman, the god of war, not unexpectedly was the Shinto deity most venerated. Houses of the aristocracy and the samurai generally contained a shrine in his honor.

Early in the sixteenth century, Yoshida Kanetomo (1435–1511), who was in charge of the imperial Shinto observances, had awakened new interest in Shintoism by attempting to assimilate elements from Tendai and Shingon Buddhism, Chinese cosmology and methods of divination. Both Nobunaga and Hideyoshi were active in rebuilding Shinto shrines for political purposes. The Inari shrine, consecrated to the goddess of food and rice, was reconstructed in 1589 by Hideyoshi who also erected handsome new buildings at Kitano. The Kamo, Kitano, and Gion shrines held annual festivals which attracted thousands of participants, and, indeed, the many festivals for which Kyoto was noted were mostly Shinto in origin. The most sacred Shinto shrines such as Ise, Izumo, and Kasuga were not in the vicinity of the capital, however. The cultural and aesthetic movements which marked the closing years of the century had little relationship with Shintoism.

Before the arrival of the Christian missionaries there were

as many as thirty Buddhist sects in Japan, but only six of these were of importance in sixteenth century Kyoto. Besides the Tendai and Shingon sects, the others were Jodo, Shin (or Ikko), Hokke, and Zen. The Tendai sect, founded by Saicho (Dengyo Daishi, 767–822) and named for T'ien-t'ai, a mountain in China where the group had its headquarters, had occupied the Enryaku-ji on Hieisan for more than eight hundred years. Even though the Tendai were Buddhists, the principal deity worshiped was a Shinto god, Sanno, identified as the nephew of Amaterasu. For many centuries lawless Tendai monks had terrorized Kyoto on innumerable occasions, fighting in the streets of the city, burning the temples, and slaughtering the adherents of rival sects. At last in the fall of 1571 Nobunaga destroyed all of the Tendai monastery buildings and killed 3,000 monks and their followers. Hideyoshi, after impounding the monastery revenues, authorized the rebuilding of Enryaku-ji but limited it to 125 temples. When the monks returned to Hieisan, they confined themselves to scholastic studies and pious works.

The Shingon (True Word) sect was introduced into Japan by Kukai (Kobo Daishi, 774–835), possibly the greatest religious figure in Japanese history, who began the huge monastic foundation on Koyasan which Nobunaga suppressed in 1581. In Kyoto the leading temple of this sect was To-ji near the old Heian city gate of Rashomon. For several hundred years To-ji was the center in the capital for the study of *mikkyo* (esoteric) Buddhism. Both Tendai and Shingon, dominating Japanese religious thought for four centuries, promised to their believers control over supernatural forces and taught that those who practiced their doctrines could become living Buddhas. Even in the sixteenth century these sects had many followers among the courtiers and aristocracy.

In the thirteenth century three new sects were founded with more appeal for the masses than the abstruse esoteric Buddhism of Tendai and Shingon. Jodo (Pure Land), instituted by Honen Shonin (1133–1212), offered rebirth in Amida's Western Paradise (Pure Land) through the repetition of the phrase "Nembutsu," a shortened form of "Namu Amida Butsu" ("Save me, Amida Buddha"). Jodo and Jodo Shin (True Pure Land) doctrines humanized Buddhism and made it comprehensible to the humblest folk. Both sects gained millions of adherents from the lower classes because worship required only faith and the repetition of the holy words. The head temple of Jodo in Kyoto was the grandiose Chion-in where Honen had initiated the Jodo reformation. In its Founder's Hall, ceremonies were publicly performed on the great holy days before thousands of worshipers enthralled by burning incense, golden decorations, and brocade vestments. The second of these sects, Ikko ("one direction" or "single mind"), more properly Jodo Shin, was organized by Honen's disciple, Shinran (1173–1262). As Jodo had simplified Tendai doctrine, so Shin simplified Jodo. To enter paradise, adherents of this sect were not even required to make the effort of belief but need only repeat the magic formula. In 1532 the Hokke sect attacked and burned the Hongan-ji, the temple of the Shin sect, and drove the Shin monks out of the city. It was the end of the century before they were able to return. In 1591 Hideyoshi gave the Shin sect the present site in Kyoto of the Nishi (Western) Hongan-ji and a large sum for building purposes. A very generous share of the sumptuous rooms from the Jurakudai and Fushimi Castle were re-erected at the Nishi Hongan-ji in the first quarter of the seventeenth century. In these gorgeous Momoyama settings the Shin services were powerfully theatrical. After Sekigahara, Ieyasu established a second Shin temple, the Higashi (Eastern) Hongan-ji, and there several immense halls were completed in 1603–1604. Both Hongan-ji quickly became leading religious centers in the capital. The third great sect was the Hokke (Lotus), instituted by the belligerent monk Nichiren (1222–82). Hokke took its name from the title of the Lotus Scripture, and its key to salvation was the prayer, "Praise to the Lotus Scripture of the Good Law." As the Hokke sect advocated worldly profits, most of the merchants who made Kyoto a prosperous commercial center in the second half of the century were believers. Hokke priests actively co-operated with the neighborhood merchant associations which took such a large share in the government of the city.

If Tendai and Shingon claimed the aristocracy and Jodo, Shin and Hokke had the greatest appeal for the common people, Zen was the sect to which the military leaders gave their allegiance. Although introduced into Japan in the seventh century, Zen made little headway until it was taken up at the close of the twelfth century by the shoguns and the *buke* class. Under the Ashikaga, Zen was practically a state religion. The Japanese word Zen (Chinese: Cha'an) was derived from Dhyana, meaning "meditation" or "contemplation" in Sanskrit. Although every Zen teacher called the essence of Zen indefinable, the purpose of Zen teaching was *satori*, illumination or enlightenment through immediate experience. There were no religious ceremonies, no teaching of doctrines or scriptures, no conventional program of study, and no worship of images. The method of the Zen master was to provoke, irritate, and exhaust the emotions of the student until he realized truth which came as a vision of enlightenment. Through contemplation the pupil had to master himself and find his own place in a spiritual universe. In contrast to the methods of the other sects, Zen insisted on salvation of the self by the self. This self-reliant character of Zen in which enlightenment was obtained through a sudden flash of intuition rather than by the study of scriptures or the strict observance of monastic disciplines appealed to the stern, unintellectual feudal warriors. It helped them to develop character and integrity by giving them the power of quick resolution and the determination to translate thought into action. Zen frugality was in accord with the conditions of a warrior's life. In awakening a deep sympathy with nature, Zen emphasized not the ever-changing face of nature but its calm serenity. A Zen garden such as Ryoan-ji was unchanging, restrained, limited, but open to an endless variety of interpretations.

In the midst of the warfare of the first half of the sixteenth century, the Zen monks stood aloof from the religious strife around them. It is impossible to overestimate the importance that Zen had for the development of poetry, ink painting, architecture, gardening, flower arranging, and the tea ceremony. The first tea seeds in Japan were planted on a hillside near Kyoto by one Zen monk, the ceramic bowls from which tea was drunk were introduced by a second Zen monk, and the teahouse as the setting for the tea ceremony was designed by a third. Moreover, before the rise of the Kyoto merchants, Zen monks kept up foreign trade with China by importing not only religious and scientific books but also the latest continental developments in textiles, painting, pottery, and other art objects. Zen monks thus occupied an extremely favorable position for assuming cultural leadership in Kyoto. Avoiding embroilment in political issues, they gained the confidence of the military rulers and acquired the funds to build the most beautiful temples and monasteries in the city. The peerless gardens at Tenryu-ji, Daitoku-ji, Ryoan-ji, and Sambo-in, the Gold and Silver Pavilions, Hideyoshi's great Daibutsu—all were in Zen temples. Most Kyoto Zen temples, including Nanzen-ji, Tenryu-ji, Daitoku-ji, and Myoshin-ji, belonged to the Rinzai branch founded by Eisai (1141–1215), who held that *satori* could come in an infinite number of ways.

By the close of the sixteenth century the upper classes were being directed away from Shinto and Buddhist views of life by a new emphasis upon the Chinese philosophy of Confucianism. Early in the Momoyama Period, Buddhism had lost much of its political and social power after the Shin and Hokke monks had been driven out of the city and Nobunaga had destroyed the Tendai and Shingon monasteries. The degeneration and disorganization of the Buddhist sects had caused the appearance of heretics and schismatics who formed new branches, preached ridiculous doctrines, and practiced depraved ceremonies. These rites were generally a combination of Shinto mysteries and Shingon occultism. With the peace and prosperity of Momoyama society, men's thoughts were turned away from the heavenly world. The arts fostered by Zen, no longer in the service of religion, were taken over into secular life. In fact, it was Zen priests who laid the foundations for the new school of Confucian ethics which became the official state cult of the Tokugawa period. The majority of the Confucianists of the early seventeenth century had once been Buddhists educated in Zen monasteries. After studying Chinese history and philosophy, they helped to transform the intellectual life of the country by substituting a Confucian rationalism concerned with the problems of maintaining social order and stability in place of the Buddhist institutions and aesthetics which had emphasized the search for salvation in another world.

The Neo-Confucian philosophy of Chu Hsi (1130–1200), the most distinguished interpreter of the Confucian classics, accorded particularly well with Ieyasu's views on administering the country. Chu Hsi's philosophy was fundamentally rational, stressing the objective reason or principle in all things as the basis for mundane learning and conduct. This idea was in striking contrast to the Buddhist view of the impermanence of the world. Another important feature of Neo-Confucianism was its emphasis upon the Five Human Relationships, the obligations between father and son, ruler and subject, husband and wife, elder and younger brother, and friend and friend, a doctrine reflected in the *gonin-gumi* system of group responsibility. Moreover, the intense nationalism and isolationism advocated by Neo-Confucianism disposed the Tokugawa Bakufu toward adopting its policy of secluding Japan from the rest of the world.

With Ieyasu's patronage, the Buddhist priest Fujiwara Seika (1561–1619) founded a school of Neo-Confucianism in which his most brilliant disciple was Hayashi Razan (1583–1657). It was mainly through the efforts of Razan, who became Confucian tutor to Ieyasu in 1608, that Neo-Confucianism was promoted as the official philosophy of the Tokugawas. Laws governing the military households, the imperial court, and the Buddhist religious communities were all drafted by Razan. Go Yozei (1570–1617), emperor during the rule of Hideyoshi and Ieyasu, expressed a contemporary view of the three religions when he wrote, "Shinto is the root of all morality, Confucianism is the branch, and Buddhism is the fruit."

The Momoyama Era falls within the so-called Kirishitan Jidai (Christian Period) which began with the arrival of Francis Xavier in 1549 and ended a century later in the persecutions with which the Tokugawa shogunate sought to wipe out every trace of Christianity. The opportunities offered missionaries to travel and preach were partly obtained because Japanese military leaders and merchants were anxious to remain on good terms with the Portuguese traders. Because the Pope had granted Portugal a monopoly on trade in the Far East, for half a century after the discovery of Japan (1542–43) only Jesuits preached there and only Portuguese merchants traded at Japanese ports. Some of the rather remarkable success of the Kirishitan missionaries was no doubt due to the degenerate condition of the great Buddhist sects. It is surprising that the Jesuits had as much initial success as they did, considering that so many Christian doctrines were utterly at variance with Buddhist teachings and practices. For example, the Japanese objected, not without reason, to a Christian theology which condemned their ancestors to damnation for never having been previously exposed to Christianity.

The description of Kirishitan activities which follows can be justified at this point not because Christianity was a major influence on Kyoto society but only because this book is written for Western readers. In the history of Kyoto the story of the missionaries is of minor consequence. After thc departure of Xavier in 1551, no Jesuits apparently visited Kyoto for more than eight years. During that time they were occupied in western Japan but always hoped to extend their mission to the metropolitan area which they had discovered was the center of government and learning.

Father Cosme de Torres, who succeeded Xavier as the Jesuit Superior in Japan, attempted to obtain permission from the abbot of Hieisan in 1555 to establish a church in Kyoto but was unsuccessful. Finally Father Gaspar Vilela (1525–72) visited Hieisan in the autumn of 1559 and through the good offices of a Tendai monk was admitted to an audience with the Shogun Yoshiteru who received him cordially and issued an order that the missionaries were to be well treated. The Buddhists, inclined at first to be tolerant of Vilela, were soon angered when they found that Kirishitan converts were forbidden to participate in any other religious rites. City officials were bribed by the Buddhists to assassinate Vilela and his Japanese interpreter, Brother Lorenzo, but they managed to escape. Rioting against Yoshiteru, however, forced them to take refuge in Sakai, leaving the capital once again without missionaries. Upon his return to the capital in September, 1562, Vilela is reported to have performed the first mass ever held in Kyoto. In 1564 he was joined by Father Luis Frois (1532–97) whose letters are a rich source of information about Kyoto in the Momoyama Period. After Shogun Yoshiteru was murdered in the early summer of 1565 by Matsunaga's troops, Matsunaga obtained an imperial rescript that the fathers were to be expelled and the church buildings confiscated. Vilela and Frois fled to Sakai once more and dared not go back to Kyoto for almost four years.

When Nobunaga captured the city in 1568, Frois returned and soon was on very familiar terms with the new ruler of the capital. The description by Frois of Nobunaga during the construction of Nijo Castle (1569) is quoted in Chapter II. Nobunaga probably welcomed the Jesuits for several reasons. He liked receiving European gifts, enjoyed hearing about the Western world and its products and inventions, and, furthermore, hated the Buddhists and was planning to destroy those sects which interfered in political affairs. In 1569 he built the missionaries a new church which became known as the Namban-ji (Southern Barbarians' Temple). When a leading Hokke monk, Nichijo Shonin, who was supervising construction of the new imperial palace, persuaded Emperor Ogimachi to issue an edict decreeing the death of Frois, Nobunaga ignored it. Frois and Brother Lorenzo later became involved in a debate with Nichijo in the presence of Nobunaga. As Frois seemed to have proved the existence of Christian immortality, Nichijo became so enraged he was restrained with difficulty from stabbing Lorenzo. Upon leaving for India in 1570, Vilela estimated that there were 150 Christians in Kyoto, a number which may be exaggerated. The bulk of the Christians in central Japan lived not in the capital but in various fortified towns whose commanders were Christian. From 1570 to 1579 the number of Japanese Christians in Kyoto increased very little, but the order considered it indispensable for prestige to have a large church in the city where all the leading Buddhist sects had elaborate temples. After the church built by Nobunaga burned in 1573, Father Organtino Gnecchi (1533–1609) drew up plans for a new three-story church which may have been in European style, at least in its interior. Whether the charming fan painting of the same period by Kano Motohide of a three-story Namban-ji in Japanese style depicts the Kyoto church is not certain. Dedicated in August, 1577, this church was to exist for only a decade.

Frois and Organtino had frequent access to Nobunaga, sometimes dining in private with him in Kyoto or at his new castle at Azuchi, sometimes receiving him for an extended visit at their seminary. During the thirteen years of his rule, he held audiences with many other missionaries, among them Alessandro Valignano, the Jesuit Visitor General, in the spring of 1581. According to the annual letter of the Jesuits in 1582, the year of Nobunaga's death and three decades after Xavier's Kyoto visit, Japanese Christians then numbered about 150,000, the majority in Kyushu. Shortly before Nobunaga's death the Jesuits were considerably disillusioned about his sincere interest in Christianity when he built a magnificent temple at Azuchi in which he was to be worshiped as a divine being.

The true religious beliefs of his successor, Hideyoshi, are unknown, but like Nobunaga he began by treating the missionaries with friendliness and consideration. Several leading Japanese Christians were close to him, including Kuroda Yoshitaku and Konishi Yukinaga, both generals in the Korean campaign; Takayama Ukon, who aided Hideyoshi in defeating the assassin of Nobunaga; the sons of the governor of Kyoto, Maeda Gen-i; Maria, the sister of Hideyoshi's consort, Yodogimi; and Magdalen, the companion of Hideyoshi's wife. For about five years relations between Hideyoshi and the missionaries were amicable.

In 1586 the Jesuit Vice Provincial Gaspar Coelho visited congregations in the Kyoto area, then numbering about 10,000 members, and called on Hideyoshi at Osaka Castle, accompanied by Father Frois who had been a friend of the Taiko for more than eighteen years. The following summer (1587) Hideyoshi invited Coelho to visit him at Hakata in Kyushu. Only a few hours after Coelho's departure, Hideyoshi issued an edict banning Christianity, commanding the fathers to leave the country within twenty days, and ordering all churches in Kyoto demolished. What Hideyoshi had seen or heard at Hakata was never known to the missionaries. All of the Jesuits except Organtino left the capital, but the edicts were not enforced, and Maeda Gen-i winked at the presence of many priests in the vicinity. By the spring of 1591 Hideyoshi, receiving Valignano in an audience, was welcoming him in his warmest and most engaging manner. At the same time Father João Rodrigues (1561–1634) was employed as Hideyoshi's official interpreter.

The Jesuit monopoly in Japan was bitterly resented by the Franciscans, Dominicans, and Augustinians who were preaching the gospel in the Philippines. In May, 1593, Father Pedro Bautista, accompanied by three other Franciscans, secured an interview with Hideyoshi at which they were granted permission to reside in Kyoto. Soon the Franciscans had built a church, mission houses, and a hospital and were openly defying Hideyoshi's 1587 proscription against preaching. Father Organtino, Ishida Mitsunari, and Maeda Gen-i all warned them of impending disaster. Kyoto was once more a flourishing center of Christianity when suddenly in 1596 an event occurred which was to bring down the wrath of Hideyoshi on the Franciscans.

The Manila galleon of that year, the *San Felipe*, on its way to Acapulco ran aground on the coast of Tosa in Shikoku, and its cargo was confiscated by the local daimyo. When one of the governors of Kyoto, Mashida Nagamori, was sent down to inquire into the situation, the Spanish captain (or pilot), according to one version of the incident, threatened him with the great power of the Spanish Empire unless restitution were made. In answer to the question of how Spain had acquired such a vast territory, the Spaniard declared that it first subdued pagan countries by Christian propaganda and then occupied them with armies aided by the converts. As soon as Hideyoshi heard this, he ordered the arrest of Father Bautista, five other Franciscans, and twenty Japanese followers. After being paraded in carts through the streets of Kyoto and dragged from city to city along the Inland Sea, the twenty-six martyrs were crucified in Nagasaki on February 5, 1597. Whether Hideyoshi was really frightened by the *San Felipe* affair is unclear. Possibly he had been surprised by the sudden revival in Kyoto of enthusiasm for Christianity. In any event, he issued another edict that all missionaries must leave the country.

The Jesuits went into hiding; probably about 100 out of 125 remained in Japan. In Kyoto, Maeda Gen-i, Ishida Mitsunari, and other influential officials protected them, but only Father Organtino, as in 1587, was allowed to remain openly in the city. Father Rodrigues was received by Hideyoshi the next year (1598) with kind words and generous gifts, and with the death of the Taiko a few days later, the enforcement of his proscriptions against Christianity ceased.

After the battle of Sekigahara (1600) had secured Ieyasu's position as military ruler, he allowed Rodrigues to build another church in Kyoto. Along with the Jesuits, the Franciscans returned to the city. According to John Saris, the Jesuits, in addition to a church, had a "very stately college" in Kyoto in 1613. The Dominicans and Augustinians opened missions in western Japan in 1602 but never established communities in the capital. While the Christians enjoyed greater freedom under Ieyasu than at any time since 1587, the number of converts was much smaller than during the decade following that year. With the removal of the administrative capital to Edo, Kirishtan activity lessened in Kyoto.

Following a series of incidents which seemed to suggest Christianity's connection with conspirators and criminals, the Tokugawa Bakufu in December, 1613, commanded Itakura, the governor of Kyoto, to draw up a list of Christians in the district. On January 27, 1614, Ieyasu issued a proclamation suppressing the Christian religion. The text of this edict has been attributed to the Kyoto Zen priest Soden and the Confucian scholar Hayashi Razan. Okubo Tadachika, the daimyo of Odawara, was charged with destroying the Jesuit and Franciscan churches in the capital and compelling the Japanese Christians to apostatize. Okubo was secretly ordered by Itakura not to kill anyone, for Ieyasu was apparently very reluctant to harm the missionaries. Nevertheless, Ieyasu was convinced that Christian beliefs were inconsistent with loyalty to the government. Because of the impending siege of Osaka, he had determined to eliminate every person who might be disloyal. The following October many missionaries and even some prominent Japanese Christians, such as Takayama Ukon, were deported to the Philippines. Although three anti-Christian decrees were published before Ieyasu's death in 1616, not one foreign missionary was executed. The situation changed completely under his son Hidetada. Persecutions grew in violence as the shoguns who followed Ieyasu set out to kill every remaining missionary and all Japanese Christians. Christianity in Japan was ended for two and one-half centuries.

It is easy to overestimate Kirishitan influence during the Momoyama Period. Whereas in other areas of Asia low-class "rice Christians" were the only converts whom the missionaries had to show for their many years of patient endeavor, in Japan several thousand people of high rank were among their followers. The total of 300,000 Christians estimated by the Jesuits at the close of the sixteenth century is an amazing figure. That these results were obtained under the military rule of Nobunaga and Hideyoshi is an indication of the tolerance of the former and the lenient enforcement of the harsh measures of the latter. The missionaries were at first objects of curiosity, then welcomed as persons whose countrymen could supply foreign commodities, especially firearms, and finally attacked as propagandists for a faith which seemed to require its adherents to be disloyal to the government and intolerant of the existing Shinto and Buddhist religions. From a historical point of view, the activity of the missionaries was only a very short episode in the long history of Kyoto. It would be difficult to demonstrate that Christianity had any important or enduring influence upon the artistic, social, or political development of the city.

5

Matsuri, Kabuki, and Other Pleasures

The people of Kyoto lived in touch with nature to a degree unimaginable among the inhabitants of the great cities of western Europe. Japanese houses with walls of sliding *shoji* which could open the entire interior to the outside placed their occupants continuously in contact with weather, birds, trees, rocks, insects, and other natural objects. Living rooms were planned to look out into landscape gardens no matter how small the available ground area might be. At every opportunity whole families went on picnics, made pilgrimages to temples, or walked to famous places to view the spring blossoms or the autumn leaves, the fireflies or the full moon. Father Rodrigues, who lived in Japan for thirty-six years, remarked that the people took "much delight and pleasure in lonely and nostalgic spots, woods with shady groves, cliffs and rocky places, solitary birds, torrents of fresh water flowing down from rocks, and in every kind of solitary thing which is imbued with nature and free from all artificiality." This love of nature tending toward melancholy was both Shinto and Buddhist in origin.

Every family had favorite trees whose annual blossoming or change of color was made the occasion for a celebration. People watched eagerly for the first wild flowers, and visited the fields or forests at the appropriate times. Spring was especially lovely at Arashiyama where the hillsides west of the city near the Katsura River had been planted with cherry trees brought from Yoshino in the thirteenth century by order of the Emperor Kameyama. There, too, were the Hozu Rapids, opened to boat traffic in 1604, and offering an exciting ride between boulders and over cascades. Well-to-do picnickers erected gaily striped tents for resting and eating, and the punctilious sent flowers to people in the neighboring tents, even though they were not acquainted. Friends exchanged poems about flowers and scenery written on long narrow strips of paper decorated in gold and silver. A sign of the democratic upheaval of the century was the mingling of nobles and commoners at picnic spots and at public entertainments. "On going out of the city one sees everywhere the loveliest and most delightful countryside of all Japan," wrote Rodrigues. "Many people go to recreate in the woods and groves of the outskirts," he continued; "every day crowds of people from the city enjoy themselves there." In summer those who were unable to go to the countryside picnicked under the willow trees along the six canals which traversed the capital or dined on platforms built out over the bed of the Kamo River. Toward evening in the fall, groups went out into the fields to listen to the plaintive chirping of grasshoppers, crickets, the "weaving insects," the "bell insects," and the "pine insects." Stretching a matting on the hillside or in the field, everyone sat quietly until late evening. To the northwest of the city, Takao was justly famous in the autumn for its scarlet maples against a dark background of cryptomerias and red pines.

Even in the middle of the city, gardens and trees surrounded the temples and shrines. When Rodrigo de Vivero y Velasco, the former Spanish governor of the Philippines, was detained in Kyoto in 1609, he was told that there were five thousand temples in the city. This figure was exaggerated, but in every neighborhood were temple gardens where people could sit under the trees or beside the ponds on the long summer afternoons when the shops were closed. Favorite afternoon walks led to the tree-embowered Chion-in, the impressive headquarters of the Jodo sect across the Kamo; the Sanjusangen-do glowing with its golden multi-headed statues of Kannon; or the great platform at Kiyomizu thrusting out toward the panorama of the capital below. A full day was required for a trip to the moss garden at Saiho-ji, the enigmatic rock garden at Ryoan-ji, or the Gold Pavilion at Kinkaku-ji.

The far-famed Kyoto *matsuri*, or festivals, which attracted visitors from all parts of the country, had originated from primitive magic rites honoring gods who were considered the sources of all natural phenomena. The year in Kyoto began in January or February with the *Toshigoi no matsuri*, the New Year's Prayer festival. Preparations were made for several days before, houses cleaned, new clothes made, and banquets cooked. Front doors were hung with pine branches, oranges, and straw ropes. On New Year's Eve people visited the Yasaka (or Gion) shrine to receive a length of burning rope lighted at the *okera* (chrysanthemum) bonfire which was used to relight the kitchen fire. The next day everyone offered greetings, paid visits, and friends exchanged gifts of toasted rice cakes and other presents. In March came the display of elaborately dressed dolls for the *Hina matsuri*, the Girls' Doll festival, observed at least since the previous century. The birthday of Buddha was commemorated in April when worshipers poured tea over the head of a statue of Baby Buddha during the *Hana matsuri* (Flower festival). The ancient *Aoi* (Hollyhock) *matsuri* held at the Kamo shrine, a May festival dating from the founding of Kyoto, had been suspended during the Onin War and was not to be revived until the late seventeenth century.

Father Ribadeneira saw the June Hachiman parade when nobles and commoners carrying arms and paper flags marched through the streets. What began as mock battles ended so frequently in casualties that Hideyoshi forbade everyone to use real weapons. From the seventeenth century on, the most popular festival with young lovers was the *Tanabata matsuri* of July 7, celebrating the one day in the year when the star called the Plowboy crossed the Milky Way on a bridge of birds' wings to meet the Weaving Maiden.

Most famous of all the Kyoto *matsuri* was the Gion festival held on July 17 and 24. The first European to describe this was Father Vilela who saw it in 1561, but it had been inaugurated in 876 and held regularly since the twelfth century except for the Onin War years. Just across the Shijo Bridge in Yasaka village was the Gion shrine dedicated to the god Susanoo, the rowdy younger brother of the sun goddess, Amaterasu. On the two days of the festival a procession of floats passed through the city streets which were decorated with lanterns and streamers. The *yama*, borne on the shoulders of young men, were tabernacles carrying sacred symbols or life-sized statues representing legendary personages. The *hoko*, named for the long pole (halberd) standing erect on the roof, were monstrous towerlike constructions draped with lanterns and rich hangings and filled with troops of musicians. Each was mounted on four huge wheels and drawn by thirty to forty men. On the *Naginata Hoko* rode a young boy in Shinto robes who was the sacred page of the deity. Between the floats marched samurai with enormous fifteen-foot-high shields of colored strips of cloth and paper strapped to their shoulders. With unrestrained drinking and dancing to the music of flutes and gongs, the two days of the Gion festival were likely to be the most joyously riotous of the whole year.

On the fifteenth of August came the *Obon*, a feast of the dead. Richard Cocks, the director of the English East India Company factory at Hirado, saw the *Obon* in 1615 and described it very accurately. "This day at night," he wrote, "all the streets were hanged with lantarns, and the pagons vizeted all their *hotoke* [idols; the word means "Enlightened One"] and places of buriall with lantarns and lamps, inviting their dead frendes to com and eate with them, and so remeaned until midnight; and then each one retorned to their houses, having left rise, wine and other viands at the graves for dead men to banquet of in their abcense, and in their house made the lyke banquet, leving part on an altor for their dead frendes and kindred." Favorite foods of the deceased were served, such as cooked sesame, eggplant, gourds, or fruit. On the third night everyone went out to the highest hills with lanterns to provide light for the souls to find their way back to the cemeteries. When the people returned to their homes, they threw rocks on the roof to drive away any souls remaining behind. This festival, introduced in Japan in 606 by the Empress Suiko, had been kept in Kyoto each year since the founding of the city.

The citizens of Kyoto were treated to many other spectacles. Burials for prominent persons were preceded by a colorful procession of mourners in white, chanting priests, and servants strewing paper flowers. At the cemetery the body was burned within a pagodalike shell as the relatives threw incense and oil onto the flames. In addition to religious observances, the capital was the setting for a series of splendid pageants staged by the military rulers to impress the emperor, daimyo and populace. In the spring of 1581 a crowd said to have numbered more than 100,000 watched the grand review of 20,000 mounted troops arranged by Nobunaga. The pageantry of Hideyoshi's entry into the Jurakudai in the fall of 1587 was easily surpassed the next year when the newly enthroned Emperor Go Yozei was invited for a ceremonial visit. The most splendid spectacle of all took place in April, 1590, when Hideyoshi set out to conquer Odawara. Sanjo Bridge across the Kamo was especially rebuilt for his departure. Each of the *giboshi* (bronze pillar bosses) on the bridge was engraved with an inscription appropriate to the occasion. Astride a horse caparisoned in gold tasseled mail with ornaments of red and green, Hideyoshi rode across the new bridge costumed in crimson laced armor, a huge gold quiver on his back and a scarlet lacquered bow in his hand. Accompanying him were generals, high officials, court nobles, and thousands of soldiers in the most brilliant display of arms and armor ever seen in the capital.

During the two decades Hideyoshi ruled in Kyoto the daily movement of nobles, samurai, ministers, and entertainers to and from the palace, the Jurakudai, and Fushimi provided the city with a constantly changing parade of elegantly robed officials, luxurious palanquins, and richly caparisoned horses and riders. After Ieyasu removed the administrative capital to Edo, Kyoto was a less colorful city. It was as characteristic of Hideyoshi that he should spend his last days in 1598 preparing a magnificent flower-viewing party and laying out the unrivaled garden at Sambo-in as it was of Ieyasu that he should die while supervising the publication of a history book and considering plans for his tomb.

The favorite entertainment of the daimyo and samurai was the dance drama called No. In the fifteenth century No ("skill" or "talent") had been the pastime of the shoguns and court aristocracy trained to recognize the classical allusions and complex verbal devices of the poetry, but in the next century Nobunaga, Hideyoshi, Ieyasu, and the daimyo who were their vassals all became ardent devotees. Hideyoshi was exceptionally enthusiastic and at times commanded performances every three or four days. He commissioned Komparu Hachiro (d. 1628), a poet and No actor, to compose new pieces on the themes of his cherry blossom party at Yoshino and his visit to his mother's memorial temple at Koyasan. After studying No dancing with the master Gosho, he appeared in performances with Maeda Toshi-ie, Ieyasu, and other lords. In a letter to his wife (1593) Hideyoshi wrote that he had learned by heart ten plays. Ieyasu made No performances a regular part of Bakufu ceremonial occasions. No stages were built by Hideyoshi at the Jurakudai and Fushimi, and wealthy daimyo erected several others in Kyoto.

No is thought to have evolved from various dances such as the *sangaku* ("irregular music"), *dengaku* ("rustic music"), and *sarugaku* ("monkey music") performed at shrines and temples in Heian times. In 1374 a Shinto priest named Kanami (1333–84) had danced a refined version of the *sarugaku* at Ima Kumano shrine in Kyoto. He was seen there by the Shogun Yoshimitsu who later became the patron of Kanami and his son Seami (1363–1444). Whether these two men actually wrote the plays attributed to them has not been proved. In any case, Seami is said to have composed ninety-three No plays and laid down the rules fixing the final form for all time. The texts which were sung melodically or intoned as recitative were based on religious or historical themes. With a small cast of two to six characters, a chorus of eight or ten, and musicians playing two drums and a flute, a No play took less than an hour to perform. Actors were masked and stiffly costumed in heavy silk and shimmering brocades. The gorgeous textiles required were partially responsible for the rapid growth of the Nishijin weavers.

The No stage was a platform (*butai*) eighteen feet square, roofed like a Shinto shrine and set in a sand-strewn courtyard. Painted on the back wall of the stage was a stylized pine tree (*matsubame*) recalling the ritual origin in a forest. The stage was attached to the dressing room by a bridge (*hashigakari*), and in front of the railing along the downstage edge of the *hashigakari* were planted three pines representing heaven, earth, and man. In the upper left corner of the stage was the "hurry door" used by the musicians, chorus, subordinate actors, and stagehands. To amplify the sound, thirteen earthenware jars were suspended beneath the stage in holes. Aristocrats and officials watched the performance from an adjacent building while commoners stood or sat on the ground.

The custom of presenting a program of five No plays in an unalterable order was fixed in the second part of the sixteenth century. The first play was about the gods, the second on the death of a warrior, the third about a woman, the fourth on a mad person, and the final play about demons. Between the No dramas were performed the *kyogen* ("wild words"), often parodies of the plays they followed. Written in colloquial dialect, they ridiculed lecherous priests, greedy daimyo, and stupid peasants. Audiences relished the sharp contrast between the serious No and comic *kyogen*.

Behind No were the teachings of Zen. The bare simplicity of the No stage, the movements of the actors based on swordsmanship, the obscure philosophy, the effects obtained by allusion or restraint, all show the influence of this Buddhist sect. No attempted to reproduce not the outward form of life but the spirit of life, thus creating *yugen*, an indefinable word frequently used by Seami suggesting "profound mystery" or "hidden meaning." The mood of *yugen* was an outgrowth of *aware*, the melancholy sadness which set the tone for so much of the court painting and poetry of the Heian Era. Typically, Seami wrote that the spectators of No sometimes found the moments of "no-action" the most enjoyable.

Kowaka dances, set to rustic music and illustrating stories of heroic adventure, were another form of entertainment enjoyed by samurai audiences. The performance is thought to have been danced by three players who recited in a highly stylized fashion. Flourishing from the middle to the end of the sixteenth century, *kowaka* is represented by about fifty extant texts of unknown authorship. This dance drama perhaps had its source in *kusemai*, melodic recitations several times longer than the usual No texts. *Kusemai* were performed in Kyoto in the bed of the Kamo River by women of low social status, but the *kowaka* were danced by daimyo and samurai. Nobunaga is supposed to have danced a *kowaka* on the eve of the fateful battle of Okehazama in 1560; Hideyoshi, Ieyasu, and Hidetada were all patrons. Hideyoshi had several *kowaka* written to eulogize his exploits. *Honno-ji* (1582) described the siege of Takamatsu, the death of Nobunaga, and Hideyoshi's punishment of Akechi.

While No and *kowaka* were preferred by the military rulers, the common people had to wait until the very end of the century for two theatrical forms which were created for lower-class tastes. These two new forms, both of which originated in Kyoto almost simultaneously, were the Kabuki, a modernized and expanded form of the No, and the *joruri*, or puppet theater. The word Kabuki is written today with Chinese ideograms which mean "song," "dance," "skill," but it has been suggested that it was derived from *kabuku*, an obsolete verb used in the Momoyama Period to mean "unusual" or "out of the ordinary" with a connotation of sexual debauchery. The date of the first Kabuki performance is usually given as 1596 when Okuni of Izumo, a Shinto priestess who is possibly legendary, performed Buddhist dances in the Kamo River bed. While there is no evidence to show exactly what her performances were like in 1596, her dance supposedly was an adaptation of the *nembutsu-odori* ("Buddha's name dance"), modified by elements of folk dancing and No movements taught by her legendary companion, Nagoya Sanzaemon.

Kabuki dance was essentially acting out the words of the narrator. Texts were adapted from No and made more understandable for less literate audiences. The visual image of the dancer in static postures was extremely significant, for the character was presented in a succession of unrelated, detached movements with no inner coherence or cumulative effect. The audience came to applaud the actor in a series of striking images. Despite the stylized dancing, the actors in contemporary clothing made the performance seem more realistic than the No plays. In Okuni's troupe women played men's roles and men played women. Okuni was so successful that in 1603, when she returned from a tour, she was invited to appear at the imperial palace. She opened a semipermanent theater in Kyoto on October 23, 1604, with a performance to raise funds for her shrine in Izumo. The unroofed platform was modeled on the contemporary No stage with a *hashigakari* extending ten to twelve feet to the dressing room. At the back of the stage was a curtain probably of vertically alternating bands of red and white. To enclose the audience a rectangular area was marked off with posts about seven feet high with straw mats hung between them. Boxes were built at right angles to the stage, but most of the playgoers sat on the ground. Between two of the posts was the single entrance over which was erected the *yagura*. Originating as a watch tower to protect aristocrats during No performances, the *yagura* became the symbol of Kabuki and an architectural feature of every theater built after 1604. Father Rodrigues observed in the first decade of the seventeenth century the many gated wooden enclosures along the roads leading into Kyoto in which were held "continuous performances of drama, comedies, farces, and plays which recount ancient stories with certain songs and tunes accompanied by musical instruments."

The second new form of lower-class entertainment which appeared in Kyoto at the same time as Kabuki was the *joruri*. About 1450, blind musicians were chanting a story called the *Tale of Joruri* to the accompaniment of the *biwa*, a four-stringed instrument somewhat like a mandolin. This narrative of a love affair between Princess Joruri and the heroic warrior Minamoto Yoshitsune became a favorite among the commoners. *Joruri*-chanting gained even more popularity with the introduction to Japan about the middle of the sixteenth century of a kind of three-stringed guitar called the *samisen* which was taken up by the blind musicians and the geisha. In Kyoto in the final decade of the century puppets were added to the *joruri*-chanting and *samisen*-playing, perhaps by a musician named Chozaburo who persuaded a puppeteer to operate wooden hand puppets while he played. In 1596 the *joruri* theater in Kyoto was evidently nothing but an open room at the end of which was a big box hiding the body of the puppet operator while his head was concealed by a curtain. The narrator chanted not only the lines but also a descriptive commentary. *Joruri*, like Kabuki, took over No plots, making them simpler to understand and more realistic. The tradition of employing masks for the No dancers and a No text recited by a chorus doubtless made it easier for audiences to accept the expressionless faces of the puppets and the chanters delivering their lines. Soon Chozaburo was commanded to perform for the Emperor Go Yozei. By the end of the seventeenth century *joruri* had become a serious art for which Chikamatsu Monzaemon (1653–1724), usually considered Japan's greatest dramatist, composed ninety-seven plays.

None of the plays written in the Momoyama Period, however, had much importance as literature. In Heian days almost all the novels, histories, poetry, and religious commentaries had been written in Kyoto by members of the aristocracy or by Buddhist priests associated with the many monasteries in the vicinity. With the breakdown of the central government, the impoverishment of the nobility, and the destruction of the monasteries, this literary activity had come to an end. In Heian times every member of the aristocracy had been expected to know by heart all of the poems in the principal Chinese anthologies, but by the period of the Korean campaign (1592) Hideyoshi had great difficulty in finding Japanese scholars competent to carry on negotiations in the Chinese language. Literature had reached one of its lowest ebbs in the Momoyama Period.

Neither the samurai nor the prosperous merchants contributed to literature, but the literary tastes of these two classes were apparent in the popularity of the bloodthirsty *gunki monogatari* (tales of war) and the grotesque *otogi-zoshi* (fairy tales). Especially popular with the samurai were histories of the great deeds of the past such as the *Taiheiki* or *Chronicles of the Peaceful Reign*, an account written in the fourteenth century by an unknown author describing the civil wars between 1181 and 1368. More than any other work it provided a foundation for a modern literary style, and the events and personages described became the themes of innumerable novels, plays, and poems. Samurai readers of Hideyoshi's time were living amid conditions which accorded only too well with those of the twelfth century. Those newly rich tradesmen and daimyo who yearned for the aristocratic refinement (*miyabi*) of the Heian Period reveled in the pictures of court life in the *Pillow Book* of Sei Shonagon (tenth century) and Lady Murasaki Shikibu's remarkable novel, *Genji Monogatari* (c. 1000). *The Tale of Genji*, one of the world's great books, was a product of purely Japanese traditions, a classic in its own day which had been devotedly read and annotated for more than five hundred years. Wealthy merchants turned to it for an understanding of *miyabi* and for a model of the extremely civilized society which they hoped to emulate. The prevailing tone of *Genji* was one of *aware* ("moving emotions," "pleasant melancholy") in large part because of a recognition of the inexorable movement of time. This Buddhist concept of life as sad and uncertain appeared inconsistent with the buoyant optimism of the Momoyama Age, yet this tinge of melancholy underlay all Japanese life and art.

The major new literary development was the *haikai*, or poetic epigram, a "free" linked-verse which in contrast to traditional poems about cherry blossoms and wan lovers delighted in mentioning "weeds, running noses, and horse dung." This simple, expansive, rather vulgar poetry had an immense appeal for warriors and commoners. *Haikai*, meaning "humor," began as an abbreviated form of the *renga*, the linked-verse which had been a court pastime since the eleventh century. During an evening of *renga*, three or more people took turns in composing verses of five, seven, and five syllables or of seven and seven syllables. In the Zen ink painting (*sumi-e*) so characteristic of the early sixteenth century, a few strokes of the brush had suggested a whole world. Similarly, in the *renga* poets sought to create with a limited number of syllables a few sharp images whose details must be supplied by the listener or reader. Eventually such elaborate rules were set up for composing *renga* that it became necessary to invent a simpler type which could be produced by ordinary people. The earliest composer of *haikai* seems to have been a Buddhist priest, Yamazaki Sokan (1445–1534). Out of the *haikai* in the seventeenth century developed the seventeen-syllable *haiku*. Master of both the *haikai* and *haiku*, Basho (1644–94) reached heights of exquisite refinement in both forms 150 years after the invention of the *haikai*.

Hideyoshi himself, although he lacked a classical education, studied poetry with the warrior-poet Hosokawa Yusai (1534–1610) and is said to have composed the following *tanka*, a thirty-one-syllable verse:

Tsuyu to oki
Tsuyu to kienan
Waga mi kana
Naniwa no koto wa
Yume no mata yume

Like dew I came,
Like dew I go.
My life,

All I have done at Naniwa (Osaka),
Is just a dream in a dream.

Ieyasu considered poetry a waste of time but devoted much attention to the collection and preservation of historical books and manuscripts. "The printing of books," he said, "and their transmission to the public is the first concern of a benevolent government." Under his patronage Kyoto became a book publishing center from the end of the sixteenth century to about 1611. In particular, he promoted the publication of books that dealt with history, economics, Confucian studies, military matters, and the administration of the empire.

With the new prosperity more commoners had leisure to amuse themselves not only with versemaking but also with such other aristocratic diversions as smelling incense, arranging flowers (*ikebana*), growing dwarf trees (*bonsai*), and designing miniature tray gardens of stones and sand (*bonseki*). A rage for playing the traditional games of *sugoroku*, a kind of backgammon; *go*, a complicated form of checkers; and *shogi*, a type of chess, swept every class. Of all the pastimes of the Momoyama Period, *cha-no-yu*, the tea ceremony, most clearly expresses the paradoxical spirit of the age. Influenced by Zen thought, everything about the tea ceremony was private, restrained, spiritual, yet under Nobunaga and Hideyoshi it became a public exhibition unparalleled in pomp and ostentation. Rich daimyo paid fantastic sums for tea jars, and Hideyoshi gave a tea party attended by thousands. "It is difficult to understand the Momoyama Age without a knowledge of *cha-no-yu*," wrote Tokutomi Iichiro in his *Kinsei Nihon Kokuminshi* (1922). "It was not only an amusement of the noble, but almost a necessity of life for the ruling class of this time. It was used as a pious device to win over men's minds. And of those who handled the empire by means of it, Hideyoshi is the most prominent example."

The initial form of the tea ritual dated from the time of the Shogun Yoshimasa (1435–90) who built the first four-and-one-half-mat tearoom at the Silver Pavilion and ordered the Zen priest Shuko to arrange the details of the ceremony. It was the Momoyama tea master (*cha-jin*) Sen no Rikyu (1521–91) who made fashionable the affectation of primitive simplicity, the pretension to refined poverty, and the admiration of beauty in the humblest household tasks. Whatever may be said about his followers, Sen no Rikyu was evidently sincere, for his four basic principles to be observed in the tea ceremony were harmony, reverence, purity, and tranquillity. His teachings popularized three words which could be applied equally well to teahouses, tea utensils, or rock gardens. *Sabi* ("mellowed") is a love for imperfection, the fallen flower, the statue with flaking paint. The steppingstones approaching the teahouse are moss covered, the tea utensils are of coarse pottery imperfectly fired, the iron kettle is old, rough, and a little rusty. Sen no Rikyu insisted that the teahouse be of the cheapest materials and that utensils be those anyone could afford. *Wabi* ("solitary") connotes frugality, rusticity, loneliness. *Shibui*, meaning "astringent," suggests artistic taste neither "too sweet nor too sour."

Sen no Rikyu not only formulated rigid rules for the tea ceremony but was a connoisseur of pottery, painting, garden stones, and architecture. The first independent teahouse (*cha-shitsu*) is thought to have been designed by him. The tea hut was set in a landscaped garden enclosed by a fence. After assembling outside at a sheltered bench, the guests approached the hut over a path of steppingstones so irregularly shaped that they were forced to watch the ground and thus become vividly aware of their surroundings. The beauty of the garden was intended to remove all thoughts of the outside world from their minds. At the entrance to the teahouse were a stone basin for washing the hands and a stone lantern. Each element was symbolic, the wick of the lantern, for example, reminding the visitor of its selflessness in being consumed in flames as it lighted the garden.

The farmhouse architecture of the teahouse was in a style called *sukiya*, from a word originally connoting "retirement to a hermitage." In Sen no Rikyu's time *sukiya* was written with ideograms which could be translated "abode of nothingness" or "house of the asymmetrical." The tearoom was entered by the *nijiriguchi* ("wriggling-in entrance"), a small door less than three feet square. In humbling himself to enter, the guest dissociated himself from the outside world. Architectural features of the interior included a crooked pillar with the bark left on, rafters of branches, walls of mud-colored clay, and ceilings of reed. In the *tokonoma* a scroll painting or vase of flowers was displayed. The host took care to dress in a kimono of subdued color which was not the same as the mounting of the painting. In the tearoom there were no social distinctions; great daimyo sat on the same *tatami* with men of inferior rank. The tea ceremony was frequently held at night in the Momoyama Period and was preceded by a frugal meal of rice, fish, and fruit. After the meal the host brought out the necessary utensils including a valuable tea caddy (*cha-ire*), if he had one, with the powdered green tea inside it. All of the bowls and other utensils were inspected and commented on by the guests as water for the tea was heating in a kettle over a fire in a square container set in the floor. The host then placed the powdered tea in a ceramic bowl using a bamboo spoon, poured hot water on it from the cast-iron teakettle, and stirred it with a bamboo whisk. The bowl of hot tea was offered first to the senior guest and then went the round of the others. As the tea was being drunk to a prescribed etiquette, the guests discussed the merits of an art object, tea bowl, painting, or flower arrangement.

In addition to Sen no Rikyu, other Momoyama tea masters were Furuta Oribe (1545–1615), who succeeded him as the supreme arbiter of taste in Kyoto, and Kobori Enshu (1579–1647), commissioner for Fushimi and probable designer of Katsura imperial villa (1624), the finest example of *sukiya* style. Apparently with the consent and encouragement of their tea masters, Nobunaga and Hideyoshi gave gigantic tea parties diametrically opposed in spirit and purpose to Sen no Rikyu's concepts. The most celebrated of these was held under the red maples at Kitano in northwestern Kyoto in October, 1587. Hideyoshi invited everybody from his richest vassals to the humblest peasants. Public announcements in Kyoto, Osaka, and Sakai requested that guests bring only a mat to sit on and a teacup. All the famous tea masters were asked to design teahouses and to exhibit their most precious tea utensils. Hideyoshi's collection of expensive tea jars was on display, and he himself served tea to some of his highest lords. Scheduled to last ten days with plays, music, and dancing, the Kitano Tea Party was interrupted when Hideyoshi had to leave to put down a revolt in Kyushu.

The crafts associated with *cha-no-yu*, such as ceramics, ironmaking, lacquer, and bamboo, all flourished, producing utensils which were very much prized and often sold for incredible prices. A tea caddy known as Tsukuno-gami

("Disheveled Hair") which belonged to Matsunaga Hisa-hide (1510–77) was valued at thirty thousand gold ducats. Hideyoshi sent Ieyasu a tea jar named Shirakumo ("White Clouds") and was in turn presented with Hatsubana ("Early Spring Flowers") whose first owner was the Shogun Yoshimasa. Ieyasu was reported to have kept eleven tea jars in the tower of Fushimi Castle guarded day and night by two soldiers.

6

The Great Decorators

Decorated with brilliantly colored paintings and intricate carvings, the buildings of Hideyoshi represented the bold, expansive character of the Momoyama Period at its zenith. In no other age did architecture, painting, and sculpture co-operate in such perfect harmony. The two unparalleled artistic achievements of the period were in the realm of painting and architecture in this new decorative style. The arts of this age were far from the Zen ideal that beauty must not be displayed but must lie modestly beneath the surface to be called forth by the connoisseur's trained taste.

The unification of the country and increased prosperity provided an opportunity to build on an unprecedented scale. In contrast to earlier ages, the most notable buildings were not religious edifices. Three new types of architecture appeared ranging from majestic castles to simple teahouses. Because of the unstable conditions which prevailed almost to the end of the century, the most distinctive architectural symbol of the age was the huge fortress castle. More significant for the centuries of peace which followed was the *shoin* style of residential architecture. The third contribution of the Momoyama Period was the *sukiya* or teahouse style discussed at length in the previous chapter in the section on the tea ceremony. These three styles were often mixed in single buildings or groups of buildings, since castles contained both *shoin* rooms and *sukiya* teahouses.

By Nobunaga's day, fortress and mansion were combined into a single architectural unity, one of the most striking products of Japanese architecture. The first of the immense Momoyama castles, Azuchi, was built by Nobunaga between 1576 and 1579. The exterior for a third of its height was massive masonry construction towering fifty or sixty feet above water-filled moats. Over these walls was a more fanciful seven-story structure of tile roofs and curved eaves piled one on the other to produce a tower almost pagoda-like in effect. Azuchi was also probably the first Japanese castle to be influenced by European ideas of fortification. Far from austere, the interiors were designed with pillars and ceilings coated in gold and red lacquer and decorated with dazzling murals by the founder of the Momoyama decorative school, Kano Eitoku. Even more impressive were the enormous castles built by Hideyoshi—Osaka (1583–86) and Fushimi (1594–96). Portions of Nijo Castle, commenced by Ieyasu in 1602, remain today.

In the Heian Period, the aristocracy lived in *shinden*-style residences consisting of pavilions connected by covered passageways surrounding and extending into a garden containing a lake for fishing and boating. Whenever the imperial palace was destroyed, it was always rebuilt in this style. *Shoin* architecture probably originated when the *shinden* pavilion was modified by certain Zen requirements. Chapels in Zen monasteries often incorporated a recessed altar with a statue of Bodhidharma and a writing desk or *shoin* at which the monks studied. Usually a window was located above the *shoin*, and shelves were built into the wall nearby. The shift to a new arrangement of rooms by partitioning the interior of the *shinden* was accomplished in the Momoyama Period. According to some theories, the recessed Zen altar became the *tokonoma* for the display of art objects, the *shoin* became a raised platform jutting into the outside corridor with a window above it, and the series of shelves placed at different levels became the *chigaidana*. The plan of a *shoin* building was rectangular with three or more rooms surrounded by a corridor and covered by a combination of hipped and gabled roof (*irimoya*). Entrance to the building was through the *genkan* ("dark space"), a porch of sufficient size for a person being carried in a palanquin to be brought under the shelter of the roof. In the main room of the dwelling the master received visitors while seated on a small platform (*jodan*), the rank of a room being indicated by the height of its floor. On the inner side of the *jodan* were usually sliding doors (*fusuma*) leading into a closet which in the Momoyama Period was used by bodyguards as a place of concealment. Ceilings in *shoin* architecture were coffered and painted, with metal fittings decorating the intersections of beams and concealing nail and bolt heads. Over the sliding doors between the rooms were carved wooden transoms called *ramma*. Solid wooden sliding rain doors (*mairado*), running on tracks parallel to the outer *shoji*, which could be closed at night or during stormy weather, were a Momoyama innovation. Everything about these *shoin* buildings contrasted with the small *sukiya* teahouses built of natural materials with a light wood frame covered by a simple bark or thatch roof.

The finest examples of *shoin* architecture existing in Kyoto today are a series of rooms which once were part of Fushimi Castle (1596), the most luxurious collection of fortified structures ever assembled in Japan. In the center of Fushimi stood the three-story *Hon-maru* (central building) surrounded by towers and mansions all with roofs of golden tiles. The name of at least one of the architects, Kora Munehiro, has been preserved. After the fall of Osaka in 1615, Fushimi was dismantled, but fortunately several of the lavishly decorated buildings were moved elsewhere.

The architectural glories of Fushimi are most apparent in the *shoin* buildings now part of the Nishi Hongan-ji. The largest room of the group, 207 feet long and 92 feet wide, was Hideyoshi's audience hall. Floored with 243 *tatami* and supported by forty-five pillars, it is divided into three sections of differing levels. At the north end is an elevated *jodan* where Hideyoshi sat. To the right of the *jodan* is a *tsuke shoin* (window-and-shelf alcove) with a dragon-decorated, coffered ceiling. The rare woods, exquisite joinery, fine plastering, and carpenter's work "as accurate as though all the parts of the building had grown together naturally" are unexcelled. The Chinese T'ang Dynasty court scene painted on the north wall of the *jodan* is by Kano Tanyu; other walls, ceilings, and sliding doors are painted with brightly colored trees, birds, and flowers by members of the Kano school. The dividing line between the *jodan* and the area for the vassal lords is stressed by a *ramma* between the levels carved with flying storks and attributed to Hidari Jingoro. West of the audience hall are three palatial rooms thought to be Hideyoshi's apartments of state. In the courtyard to the north is a No stage formerly at Fushimi.

The Nishi Hongan-ji also possesses an exceptional example of a Momoyama gate from Fushimi. Named the Chokushimon (Imperial Messenger Gate), it is a fine specimen of a *karamon* (Chinese gate) with great curved gable roofs at front and rear called *kara-hafu* (Chinese gables). On the lintel a peacock spreads its tail, tigers crouch on the beams, and lions romp among peonies with such an abundance of other animals and flowers both real and imaginary that it is popularly known as *Higurashi no mon* (Livelong Day Gate) because the viewer might well spend a day studying its amazing sculptured detail.

At Nijo Castle the first three of five connected buildings of the *Ni-no-maru* (secondary castle compound) are probably from Fushimi. Like the rooms at Nishi Hongan-ji, these are beautiful examples of the *shoin* style. Among the most spectacularly decorated chambers are the Imperial Messenger Room, the Shikidai where presents for the shogun were received, and the Ohiroma (Audience Hall for the Outer Lords), all intended to dazzle visitors with highly colored paintings of pines, bamboos, and birds against gold backgrounds and polychrome *rammas* carved with phoenixes and peonies. The connecting corridors have "nightingale" floors designed to squeak when walked on. Everything about the *Ni-no-maru* is larger than ordinary; the columns are wider than usual and ornamented with gilded hardware almost rococo in its curves; the ceilings are double coffered and compartmented; and Japan's largest paintings, massive designs by Kano Sanraku and Kano Tanyu, adorn the walls. Only in the shogun's private apartments are there restrained, fragile landscapes. Of the many structures erected at Nijo by order of Ieyasu, the main gate supported by huge stones, with heavy doors and beams protected by bands of metalwork, remains. The most striking aspect of the exterior of the *Ni-no-maru* is the tiled *irimoya* roofs with flamboyant chiseled gold bronze strapwork on the gable ends.

Most opulent of the Momoyama mansions was the Jurakudai, completed by Hideyoshi in 1587. The main entrance was through a two-story iron gate embellished with metal birds, beasts, and plants. Emerald green and gold-plated tiles covered the roofs of *shoin*-style pavilions. According to the 1625 biography of Hideyoshi, the *Taikoki*, "the pattern of the tiles was like jewelled tigers breathing in the wind, and like dragons intoning in the clouds." The Jurakudai was demolished by Hideyoshi after the death of Hidetsugu (1595), but a gate comparable to the Chokushimon was given to the Daitoku-ji. In addition, Hideyoshi's lakeside villa from the Jurakudai, the Hiunkaku (Flying Cloud Pavilion), was re-erected at the Nishi Hongan-ji. This is the only existing building from the Momoyama Period which successfully combines the *shoin* and *sukiya* styles. The roof is a unique but harmonious blending of *irimoya*, *kirizuma* (gable), and *shichu* (hip). Inside, the Hiunkaku contains intimate *shoin* rooms, an embarkation chamber for entering a boat on the lake, and Hideyoshi's bathroom with morning glories painted by Kano Eitoku. On the top floor is a celebrated painting of Fuji attributed to Kano Motobonu with pine trees at the bottom said to have been mischievously added by Hideyoshi himself. A number of *sukiya*-style teahouses remain from the Momoyama Period. One from the Jurakudai is now at the Sambo-in and two from Fushimi at the Kodai-ji. A fourth now at Kennin-ji was exhibited by a pupil of Sen no Rikyu at the famous Kitano Tea Party (1587).

Whereas innovations in architecture, painting, and sculpture had previously appeared first in Buddhist monasteries and temples, in the Momoyama Period the building of religious edifices was largely confined to the restoration of ruined temples and shrines according to the original plans. The most splendid new temple was the Hoko-ji, where Hideyoshi constructed the gigantic Daibutsu-den. The buildings of the Hoko-ji presented no new architectural developments, however, for the architects, Nakamura Masakiyo and Heinouchi Yoshimasa, were ordered to copy ancient Chinese styles. The Zen temple of Kodai-ji, built by Hideyoshi's widow in 1604, was one of the few temples in the style of the period. The buildings which exist today display the same vermilion lacquered pillars, carved polychrome ornaments, and shining metal fittings to be found in Momoyama castles. The Kitano shrine, begun by Hideyoshi and completed in 1607 by Hideyori, has a very complicated roof named *yatsumune* (eight roofs) required by the *gongen* style in which the oratory and sanctum are joined under one voluminous roof but separated within by the *ainoma*, a sunken room paved with stone.

Primarily because of the decreasing patronage of Buddhism, sculpture which had been entirely in the service of religion declined in importance. Images were still supplied for the almost depopulated monasteries, but the work was done by craftsmen, not artists. Painters, instead of sculptors, were patronized by the military rulers who needed the vast rooms of their castles and palaces covered with large scale murals. When Hideyoshi resolved in 1587 to erect a bronze Buddha larger than those at Nara or Kamakura, two brothers from Nara, Teiso and Soin, experts in making Buddhist statues, were chosen as consultants. The metalworkers had lost their ability, however, and after several failures to cast the statue, a Chinese sculptor was hired to fashion an image 160 feet tall out of wood covered with lacquer made from oyster shells.

The most successful sculpture of the early sixteenth century consisted of the No and *kyogen* masks which combined abstract symbolism with the realistic portrayal of different types. Primitive masks had been used for dances as early as the ninth century, but the No mask makers imbued their masks with an ambivalent quality whereby a simple mask could serve to evoke joy or anger, happiness or grief, according to the pantomime of the actor. Inspired by Zen teaching, these masks shared the tendency shown in teamaking, gardening, and pottery to organize art as though it were ritual. Generations of carvers brought the making of No masks to its artistic height in the Momoyama Period.

Despite his construction of the Daibutsu, Hideyoshi cared little for religious sculpture but needed a vast amount of carving as architectural decoration in his palaces. Sculptors enriched his residences with carved transoms, friezes, gables, beams, and paneling in such intricate shapes that spectators truly stood in amazement. Sculptural work on *ramma*, *kibana* (beam ends), and *kaeru-mata* (brackets) reached the peak of its development. Men, birds, animals, and flowers observed from nature were carved with astonishing accuracy and realistically colored–a realism in striking contrast to the subtlety and elimination of the obvious which had characterized the Buddhist-inspired sculpture of previous ages. The name of Hidari ("left-handed") Jingoro (c. 1594–1634), considered Japan's greatest wood carver, is linked with the decoration of Fushimi, Nijo, and almost all the skillful and ornate carvings of the Momoyama Period. As Fushimi was completed in 1596 and Nijo begun in 1602, many of these attributions must be legendary. Some of the incredibly fantastic carvings on the shrine of Ieyasu at Nikko (1617–36) are considered examples of Hidari's later work.

The second great contribution of the Momoyama Period was in the area of decorative painting. Many Japanese critics regard this vigorous, complex painting as the most original and creative of all Japanese art styles. At the beginning of the sixteenth century there were two general styles of painting, the Yamato-e or Japanese and the Kara-e or Chinese. The Yamato style was exemplified by the traditional paintings of the Tosa family. The ancient Chinese techniques and subject matter were transformed by members of the Kano family into the opulent Momoyama style. The Tosa school was delicate, feminine, owing hardly anything to Chinese influence; the Kano school stood for Chinese ideals, modified by Japanese sensibility and the love of sumptuous display of the newly rich and newly powerful. The prosperous merchants had a very free and matter-of-fact view of life and were not interested in classical subject matter but in the more vital civilization of their own time. As they gained in social as well as economic influence, a new genre painting appeared. The pleasures of the common people—flower viewing, sightseeing, picnics, horse racing, music, dancing, the stage, street scenes of the commercial areas with craftsmen working in shops—were all good subjects for the genre painters. Even the great Kano Eitoku painted screens illustrating "Rakuchu-Rakugai" (Kyoto city and suburbs). Kano Hideyori's screen "Maple Viewers at Takao" and Kano Motohide's "Rakuchu-Rakugai" fan-papers are genre sources for information about the everyday life of the era. From this genre painting evolved the remarkable Ukiyo-e ("floating world pictures") of the later seventeenth century.

What was new about Momoyama painting, however, was its huge size and brilliant color. The expansive paintings of this period were known as *shohekiga* (paintings on walls, doors, or screens) in contrast to the smaller *kakemono* (vertical scrolls) and *makimono* (horizontal scrolls) of previous centuries. Artists had to paint on this large scale to match the dimensions of the innumerable rooms in the new castles and palaces. Walls and screens were covered with full-scale pine trees, blossoming plums and cherries, banks of irises and chrysanthemums, fantastic rocks, brightly plumaged birds, crouching tigers, and undulating dragons, all against shimmering backgrounds of gold or silver, lapis lazuli blue, and malachite green. One of the most striking features was this use of gold leaf which reflected light into the dark interiors and outlined the silhouettes of painted trees, animals, and men. Thus the gold backgrounds, hard outlines, and flat designs of the Kano style were devices for overcoming the dull visibility in rooms darkened by Kyoto's cloudy, rainy weather and eight-foot roof projections. This new style in which strong, black Chinese brush stroke outlines were filled in with the flat, bright colors of Yamato-e was founded by Kano Masanobu (*c.* 1434–*c.* 1530), firmly established by his son Motonobu (1476–1559), and reached its height in the work of his greatgrandson, Kano Eitoku (1543–90).

The first grandiose examples of this style were painted by Eitoku when he decorated five of the seven stories of Azuchi Castle in 1576. After the destruction of Azuchi, Hideyoshi had Eitoku decorate Osaka Castle (1583–86) and the Jurakudai (1586–87). Assisted by his eldest son, Mitsunobu (1565–1608), and his son-in-law, Sanraku (1559–1635), Eitoku produced work on a scale and in quality greater than anything done before. With the patronage of both Nobunaga and Hideyoshi, Eitoku must have been the busiest, as well as the most prosperous, artist of his time. The enormous murals in castles and mansions ascribed to Eitoku were probably joint works by as many as ten artists. Eitoku and his assistants were in charge of composing general ideas, drawing rough sketches, and painting finishing touches. Existing authentic works by Eitoku are very few. Two remaining screens hint at the glory of the *shohekiga* lost in the burning of Azuchi and dismantling of the Jurakudai. On an eight-fold screen a massive cypress tree, sculpturally modeled, is shown almost life size. As the tree is cut off above the roots and below the tops of the branches, the sense of magnitude is increased in the mind's eye. The coloring, too, is lifelike with the texture of the branches graphically presented. In the background are gold clouds and azurite blue water. Another superb work is an eight-foot-high six-panel screen of two *karashishi* (imaginary lions) painted in rich browns and greens against gold leaf.

After Kano Eitoku's death in 1590 several followers carried on his work, notably Kano Sanraku, his son-in-law, who became the leader of the Kyo-Kano or Kano school in Kyoto. Sanraku was such a favorite with Hideyoshi that the latter had asked Eitoku to adopt him and give him the Kano name. In his work, less bold than that of Eitoku, trees, rocks, and animals are painted in a detailed, naturalistic style against the usual golden backgrounds. At Myoshin-ji is a room with strange, imaginary tigers in a vivid green bamboo grove, and Daikaku-ji in western Kyoto has a magnificently composed plum tree with its branches extending over eight *fusuma*. With Sanraku the brilliant Kano style was nearing its end in the capital.

Mitsunobu, the eldest son of Eitoku, painted for Hideyoshi and later Ieyasu, but far more important was Kano Tanyu (1602–74), the grandson of Eitoku, who was clever enough to leave Kyoto and go to Edo where he gained the favor of Ieyasu. Becoming the official artist for the shogunate in 1617 when he was not quite sixteen years old, he established the academic art standards which all seven generations of the Kano family were to follow. Among the many works in Kyoto ascribed to him are typical Kano-style wall and sliding-door paintings at Nijo, Nanzen-ji, Nishi Hongan-ji, and Daitoku-ji.

While the Kano family held the central position in the world of art, there were many other artists competing with one another. Unkoku Togan (1547–1618) called himself the successor of Sesshu (1420–1506) and, like that supreme genius of the fifteenth century, tried to suggest in unusually bold monochrome ink painting (*suiboku*) the richness of the visible world without actually copying it. Kaiho Yusho (1533–1615), having at first learned from Kano Eitoku, developed his own style of polychrome painting in which black became as vibrant as color. He was probably one of Eitoku's many assistants at the Jurakudai. Of his four six-panel screens owned by the Myoshin-ji, one with realistically drawn pink and white peonies is perhaps the most beautiful.

Also active outside the Kano school was Hasegawa Tohaku (1539–1610) who painted a series of panels at Chishaku-in (1591) with sharp, spirited brush strokes and opaque earth and mineral colors. More admired today are a pair of six-panel screens painted in *sumi* (black ink) on semiabsorbent paper in the manner of Sesshu. With daring conciseness and bold spacing he suggests pine trees in a swirling, misty rain. The ink wash spreading on the absorbent paper produces an astonishing effect of mist and fog more poetic in atmosphere than anything in the standardized Kano-school paintings. In a similar soft, blurred style are the monkeys and trees in his screen at the Shokoku-ji.

The Tosa family, hereditary artists to the court, continued to paint in the distinctly Japanese style of Yamato-e showing Japanese customs and scenery rather than those of classical China. One of the greatest names in the early sixteenth century was that of Tosa Mitsunobu (1434–1525), whose daughter married a member of the Kano family, Motonobu. In the Momoyama Period, Tosa Mitsunori (1563–1638) drew in a fragile, sinuous ink line following fourteenth-century models. This refined, delicate line of the Tosa school seldom looked sufficiently strong in *sho-hekiga*, especially if compared with the firm black boundary lines of the Kano painters. Yamato-e was a declining tradition until it was given new life by the very original treatment of Tawaraya Sotatsu (1576–1643). He lived at Takagamine, a community of artists founded by the versatile Honami Koetsu, and probably owed the inspiration for his humorous treatment of classical subjects to the eminent men of taste who were attracted there by Koetsu. Sotatsu is especially distinguished for his use of *tarashikomi* coloring, obtained by dripping pools of pigment on wet colors. This technique of spreading and blending colors was adopted by the greatest painters of the second half of the seventeenth century. Sotatsu depicted almost exclusively the deities, demons, and noble personages who had appeared in the paintings of the Fujiwara (894–1185) and Kamakura (1185–1333) periods.

It is evident that these creative trends in painting were not the work of one individual or of one family school, for the age embraced both the austere understatement of *sumi* ink painting and the lavish, colorful profusion of the Kano murals. In size and splendor these wall and screen paintings were quite in keeping with the boundless ambitions of the military rulers. Yet even at their most sumptuous, they never degenerated into mere vulgarity, for both Nobunaga and Hideyoshi, although not aristocrats, had the good sense to surround themselves with the very greatest architects, artists, and craftsmen.

Kyoto as the center for the tea cult became the leading producer of the tea ceremony ceramics. According to many connoisseurs, the experimentation by Japanese potters and the introduction of Korean techniques made the Momoyama Period the most significant in the history of ceramic art in Japan. The most famous Kyoto tea ceremony bowls are called Raku (pleasure), a name derived from the second component of Hideyoshi's Jurakudai (Palace of Pleasure). The prestige of Raku ware was due to Sen no Rikyu who selected this type of simple Korean peasant rice bowl for his tea rituals. Raku ware was first made in Kyoto prior to the mid sixteenth century by Ameya, a Korean potter who had settled in the capital and married a Japanese woman, Teirin. After his death, she continued to make this Korean style pottery. Her son Chojiro (1515–92), traditionally supposed to have used clay from the premises of Jurakudai, was honored by commissions from Nobunaga who followed the advice of Sen no Rikyu. To Chojiro's son Jokei was granted the gold seal bearing the character *raku* which henceforth appeared on the bottom of every bowl. Japanese critics have acclaimed the Raku ware of Chojiro's grandson, Donyu (1599–1656), as the finest of all.

Raku tea jars and bowls appeared unimpressive to foreign visitors, but it was this rustic simplicity which recommended Raku to Sen no Rikyu. Great care was exercised in shaping and glazing the bowls to make them as free from artificiality as possible. The clay was coarse, the shape of the bowls irregular, and spatula marks were not smoothed out. When the glaze was applied, it was allowed to flow down unevenly and stop in wavy lines. Natural accidents in firing in the little two-foot-square ovens often marred the glaze. The qualities of Raku admired by the tea masters were these variations in texture, the feeling of softness in the hand, and the thickness which prevented the outside from becoming too hot. Tea votaries praised the beauty of the clay paste and could tell which kiln it came from by its color and coarseness. Several types of tea bowls were made, a large bowl for thick, pasty tea, a smaller one for thin, foamy tea, shallow bowls for summer, heavy bowls for winter. Three different colored glazes were used: *kuro* (black), heavy and brownish; *aka* (red), a reddish orange; and *shiro*, a thick white. Actually a highly elaborate technique and great skill were required to obtain the effect of naturalness. Reflecting as it does the character, personality, and temperament of the maker, Raku has always been considered the most typically Japanese of all native wares.

When the tea cult spread from the aristocracy to the samurai and merchants, the increased demand for tea utensils had caused Japanese potters in Seto, near present-day Nagoya, to imitate imported Chinese and Korean ware. Seto pottery became so popular in Kyoto that Nobunaga made the rounds of the Seto kilns in 1574 designating six master potters. Seto ware was called Shino, a heavy coarse type with creamy white glaze decorated with simple designs in reddish iron oxide.

In the late sixteenth century the Seto potters began to make green glazed Oribe ware, a type supposed to have originated with Furuta Oribe, the successor of Sen no Rikyu as supreme arbiter of taste. Seto wares began to take on new aspects with experiments in underglazing, an opaque yellow glaze, and light brown patterns. Seto potters came to Kyoto and, opening a kiln in Awata at the foot of Higashiyama, produced tea jars and bowls called Kyo-yaki (capital ware). Many potters settled at Mizoro about four miles northwest of the capital and others at Fushimi and in the Yasaka and Otowa districts. Kilns were founded on the hillside near Kiyomizu where there is a street of potters to this day ("Teapot Lane"). At this time a method of overglaze enameling introduced from China led to the development of a distinctive new line of Kyo ware reflecting the Momoyama love of brilliant color.

Potters who were captured in Hideyoshi's Korean campaigns brought with them the secrets of porcelain manufacture. When porcelain stone of fine quality was discovered in Hizen Province in Kyushu, numerous factories were built there. Meals for all classes had been served in wood and lacquer bowls, but with the introduction of Japanese porcelain, fashionable Kyoto aristocrats and merchants began to eat from delicate porcelain dishes. Even though the ceramic industry was dispersed into several provinces, Kyoto remained the gathering place for ceramic artists. Just as the Nishijin weavers had made Kyoto the leading city in cloth manufacturing, so the potters who settled in the capital from all over the country made it the center of the ceramic industry.

Other applied arts flourished in the capital because of the presence of famous artists and tea masters. It was a time when masterpieces were created in lacquer ware, metalwork, and wood and ivory *netsuke*. Momoyama lacquer was unequaled in such qualities as hardness, durability, and bold design. Although porcelain manufacturing had been established, a hundred years were to elapse before it became a rival of lacquer. A purely Japanese invention in lacquer ware was a technique called *maki-e* in which powdered gold, silver, or copper was sprinkled on a lacquer ground. It was usually called Kodai-ji *maki-e*, for the finest examples were to be found in the temple of that name built by the widow of Hideyoshi (1604). The leaves of the door to the shrine containing the statues of Hideyoshi and his wife were decorated with *maki-e* panels showing pampas grass and chrysanthemums on one side and paulownia, pine, and bamboo on the other. Letter and writing boxes, book-stands, and tiny medicine boxes (*inro*) were all richly decorated in *maki-e* technique combined with carved lacquer, cut gold and silver, sheet gold, and mother-of-pearl. Another Momoyama development was the revival of painting on lacquer. Gay and worldly designs were painted in red, yellow, green, and black on brilliant red backgrounds. These designs looked nonchalantly drawn, but in reality they were flawlessly planned. Many lacquer articles designed for export to Europe were produced in Kyoto, including an extant backgammon board which shows Kiyomizu shrine.

Until the Momoyama Period, sword mounts had been most valued when they were functional, but with Hideyoshi the custom began of making collections of inlaid, enameled, and *repoussé* work sword ornaments. The Goto family, famed for its intricately designed ornaments, devoted particular attention to the *menuki* (rivet) which was placed under the hilt to improve the grasp. A master of inlay work, Goto Tokujo (1549–1631), belonging to the fifth generation, was presented an estate by Hideyoshi in 1580. A talented member of another family of metal workers, Umetada Myoju produced delicately chiseled inlay and pierced work sword guards which have never been surpassed. The demand for iron kettles for the tea ceremony brought about the establishment in Kyoto of several families which specialized in making them. Nagoshi Yashichiro served Nobunaga in this way, and his son Yaemon cast the giant bell for the Daibutsu-den used as the pretext for the controversy between Ieyasu and Hideyori. Tsuji Yojiro, who worked for Sen no Rikyu and Hideyoshi, was noted for the technical refinement and elegant form of his kettles. The Momoyama fondness for large-scale decorations was never more brilliantly apparent than in the bronze metal fittings which curved and twined along ceilings and rafters, over the upper and lower ends of columns, and across gables.

Fashion dictated that gentlemen should suspend tobacco pouches, pipe cases, purses, and *inro* from their girdles with silken cords. These cords were passed through a button or toggle called *netsuke* ("to fasten the end"). Deities, demons, animals, scenes from everyday life, and all sorts of objects were depicted on *netsuke* which were carved from wood, ivory, or bone in high or low relief. Such endless effort was expended on carving these *netsuke* that each tiny button became a work of art.

Certainly the most versatile genius in the applied arts was Honami Koetsu (1558–1637). The son of a family whose judgment on swords was regarded as infallible, he is said to have learned the tea ceremony from Furuta Oribe and Raku pottery making from Jokei. In fact, the Raku ideogram with which this pottery was signed was an example of Koetsu's calligraphy. Regarded as one of the three finest calligraphers of his time, he was no less skilled in painting, lacquer work, landscape gardening, engraving, wood carving, and Japanese poetry. In 1615 when Ieyasu presented Koetsu with an estate at Takagamine on the northwestern outskirts of Kyoto, he retired there with fifty-five friends and relatives. His village of craftsmen became a renowned haven of culture and attracted illustrious painters, wealthy merchants, and great daimyo. Koetsu was only one among many amazing Momoyama craftsmen who excelled in a great variety of fields.

Among the many temple gardens in the vicinity of the capital which still retain their sixteenth-century form, not one of Hideyoshi's gardens has been left intact. Only at the Sambo-in near a quiet village about two miles from Fushimi does a garden exist just as it was laid out by Hideyoshi. In the spring of 1598 the most famous cherry-viewing party in the history of Japan was held by Hideyoshi near the temple of Daigo-ji. His camp, which was pitched on Hanami-yama (Flower-viewing Hill), was enclosed by one hundred gold-leaf screens decorated with the imperial *kiku* (chrysanthemum) and *kiri* (paulownia). Hideyoshi was so charmed with the nearby temple of Sambo-in that he ordered extensive restorations to the buildings and the construction of the most famous of all Momoyama gardens.

The greatest glory of this garden is its stones which are without equal. Where Ryoan-ji has fifteen rocks, Sambo-in has more than eight hundred, each selected with infinite care and many so highly regarded that while being transported to the site they were wrapped in brocade to avoid damage to the weathered surfaces. Rocks brought from long distances were accompanied by attendants whose duty it was to water the stones periodically to prevent the moss or lichen from withering. The most celebrated stone in all Japan is at Sambo-in, the Fujito-no-ishi. Roughly rectangular in shape with a weathered patina, it came from the straits of Fujito, the scene of a battle between the Taira and Minamoto in 1184 which later became the subject of a No play. After many years in various Kyoto gardens, the Fujito stone was transported in state to the sound of music and set up at Sambo-in. There in about one acre the hundreds of rocks are arranged so that the qualities of each are fully displayed without lessening the overwhelming effect of splendor.

Sambo-in is truly representative of the age, for it combines the three main types of Momoyama gardens. On a larger scale than anyone but Hideyoshi could afford, this garden incorporated an expansive *shinden* lake garden, a Zen *karesansui* in which mountains and rivers were represented symbolically, and a *roji* ("dewy path") garden designed as usual to dissociate the teahouse from the outside world. In the lake garden are boldly shaped trees and bushes grouped around twisting areas of water fed by two partially hidden waterfalls. Three traditional Chinese "tortoise," "crane," and "paradise" islands are linked by bridges, two of stone and one of wood topped by moss-covered earth. At one side of the *shoin*-style mansion is a small *karesansui* garden of gravel containing three different stones arranged as in a Sung ink painting. Sambo-in is an exquisite example of the fusion of garden, mansion, and paintings into a single aesthetic unit. The design of the garden is attributed to Asagiri Shimanosuke who had planned the gardens at Fushimi. Hideyoshi never saw the Sambo-in garden completed, for he died in September 1598. Kentei, the head gardener, continued to work on it for the next twenty-six years.

A second existing Momoyama garden is the Tiger Glen (Kokei), once part of Fushimi and now at Nishi Hongan-ji. In an area of about sixty-five feet by ninety-five feet a wild mountain glen with a large dry cascade has been built. Among the plantings are semitropical sago palms admired by Hideyoshi, an exoticism affirming the outreaching spirit of the age. A third Momoyama garden lies to the west of the *Ni-no-maru* at Nijo Castle. Resembling Sambo-in, the stones of this garden are even larger, more numerous, and more irregular. The design is attributed to the Zen tea master Kobori Enshu. For many people, this massive, formal set piece crowded with too many rocks epitomizes the cold pomposity of the Tokugawa shogunate for which it was constructed.

7

Epilogue

By the second quarter of the seventeenth century, Kyoto was slipping quietly into a long process of decline which was to continue for more than two hundred years. When Edo had been made the military capital of Japan in 1603, Kyoto was still the largest city and the mercantile center of the empire. But in the next half century not only did the old capital suffer a loss of population and revenue as all of the Bakufu officials were moved to the new city, but its manufacturing and commerce began to languish with a depression in the Nishijin textile industry and the destruction of foreign trade when Japan closed its doors to the outside world.

The population was further reduced when the Shogun Iemitsu (1622–51) instituted a device in 1635 called the *sankin-kotai* ("alternate attendance") system. Hideyoshi had required various daimyo whose loyalty he suspected to live in Kyoto where they were forced to spend their incomes erecting luxurious mansions and taking part in court activities. This scheme was employed by the Kampaku with such cleverness and tact that there was not a single revolt against him after 1590. Hoping to devise a similar system that would hold in check the ambitions of the most powerful lords, Iemitsu decreed that all daimyo, Fudai and Tozama alike, were obliged to spend four months of every other year in Edo. Fiefs had been distributed to the Fudai daimyo in such a way that the shogun's loyal vassals could keep watch on the doubtful Tozama daimyo even during the alternate years when the Tozama were not in Edo.

Determined that the provincial lords should have no opportunities to intrigue with one another or with the imperial court in Kyoto, the Tokugawas forced all the daimyo to bring their wives and children to live permanently in Edo, and even the sons of the chief samurai were kept in the military capital as hostages. Eventually all the great lords built extravagant mansions there and, in consequence, no longer spent part of each year in Kyoto. As early as 1614, William Eaton of the English East India Company, having experienced difficulty in selling cloth in Kyoto, complained that "all the gentlemen are gone to Edo." Even the shoguns themselves no longer appeared in their western capital. After only a single visit by the shogun in nine years, Nijo Castle, the symbol of Kyoto's occupation by outsiders, was once more the setting for a lavish entertainment when in August, 1634, Iemitsu arrived with an army of 300,000 which had been assembled to overawe the citizens with the power and splendor of the Tokugawas. Following a brief visit, Iemitsu returned to Edo, and almost 230 years were to pass before another shogun set foot in the old capital.

Although Ieyasu's policy had been to make Edo not only the military and administrative capital but also the economic and cultural center of Japan, Kyoto culture continued to prevail in the early years of the Edo Period. All of the craftsmen, for example, who designed and decorated the vast and ruinously extravagant castle of Edo erected by the daimyo for Ieyasu between 1600 and 1614 were brought from Kyoto. While Ieyasu and his successors were establishing the new government in Edo, the great provincial daimyo, eager to patronize the arts, were bringing Kyoto painters, sculptors, potters, weavers, musicians, and actors to their country estates and thereby spreading Kyoto culture to the remotest corners of the empire.

In Kyoto the supreme architectural achievement of the seventeenth century was the Katsura imperial villa, a deceptively simple country mansion commenced by Prince Toshihito in 1620 on the west bank of the Katsura River. The simplicity and restraint of this beautiful house is in striking contrast to the overdecorated palaces and temples being built by the Tokugawas in Edo and Nikko at the same time. Under the Tokugawas the carved wood decorations so characteristic of the Momoyama style degenerated into jungles of contorted bracketing as all functional form disappeared under useless ornaments and flamboyantly colored details. If the Toshogu shrine at Nikko (c. 1636) and other Tokugawa buildings were not in questionable taste, it was because they managed to retain an intrinsic Japanese elegance even when all traditional restraint and understatement were lost. This establishment at Nikko of the cult of Ieyasu and the Tokugawa family, together with the official revival of Confucianism with its insistence upon loyalty and orthodoxy, was intended to counteract any insidious, disintegrating tendencies that might emanate from the great Buddhist foundations in Kyoto. But although worshipers continued to throng the spectacular festivals at Kyoto shrines and temples, the monks were politically impotent and Buddhism seemed almost to vanish from the historical scene.

Traditional art forms were kept alive by members of the 130 noble families living in Kyoto who, having no other source of income, had to earn a living by teaching painting, music, poetry, calligraphy, or deportment. Yet classical poetry was dead, the once fashionable *renga* replaced by even more irregular verse forms, and the tea ceremony degenerating into an empty ritual. Even though the high quality of Kyoto tea ceremony bowls began to slacken and become mannered as the century passed, many ceramic artists still found the atmosphere of the old capital stimulating. Among these were Ninsei (1596–1660) and Kenzan (1663–1743); both created superbly crafted jars and bowls enameled in sophisticated patterns. The last of the great Kyoto painters was the brother of Kenzan, the incomparably versatile Korin (1658–1716) whose startling designs on bowls, robes, and screens recalled the exuberant compositions and vivid color contrasts of the Momoyama Age.

Among the performing arts, the puppet play, having originated in the old capital, was to reach its height in the melodramas of the great Chikamatsu (1653–1724), staged in the burgeoning commercial city of Osaka, and Kabuki, also a Kyoto creation, was to attain its greatest success in Edo. By mid-century, Japanese writers acknowledged that Edo had attracted to itself most of the learning and talent and had become the center of a new cultural sphere.

With an embargo on foreign trade, Kyoto's mercantile fortunes were also waning. During the rule of Iemitsu, Japan was hermetically sealed from the outside world by a series of edicts which expelled the Spaniards (1624), the Portuguese (1639), and in 1640 all other foreigners except authorized Chinese and a few Dutch traders confined to tiny Deshima Island in Nagasaki Harbor. After 1637, Japanese were forbidden to leave the country, and any who did were executed if they attempted to return. Osaka, commanding the land routes to the east and the Inland Sea routes to the west, replaced Kyoto as the major trade center. The wealth accumulated by Kyoto merchants in the sixteenth century did not disappear immediately, but the city was further impoverished about the middle of the century when two large conflagrations destroyed much of the Nishijin area. The weavers were unable to recover their former prosperity, and Nishijin lost its leadership in the textile industry to Edo. Even the gay quarters of Shimabara declined until only about a dozen houses remained open.

Although its political, religious, and artistic supremacy had ended, for the next two centuries Kyoto was to remain the goal of countless poets and painters, travelers and pilgrims who came to worship at its venerable shrines, to stroll along willow-bordered canals, to wander in silent ravines, to delight in the surging life of the markets, and perhaps, in the long weeks of autumn when the warm haze lay over Higashiyama and wild chrysanthemums bloomed under the golden maples and crimson sumacs, to dream of the glorious days of the sixteenth century.

Selected Bibliography

The Capital

Hürlimann, Martin. *Kyoto.* New York, 1961. Attractive photographs.

Mosher, Gouverneur. *Kyoto: A Contemplative Guide.* Tokyo, 1964. A pleasant guide to existing castles, temples, and gardens with much helpful, accurate information.

Osaragi, Jiro, Takehiko Ibuki, Minoru Shibata, *et al. Kyoto.* Kyoto, 1962. Beautiful photographs and lively introductory essays in English on Kyoto's history, arts, festivals, and people.

Ponsonby-Fane, R. A. B. *Kyoto: The Old Capital of Japan.* Kyoto, 1956. Part Three contains a description of all Kyoto buildings in the Momoyama Period based on a careful search of Japanese documents. Indispensable.

History and People

Azuchi-Momoyama Jidaishi Ron. Tokyo, 1915. Twelve essays by leading scholars. In Japanese.

Cooper, Michael (editor). *They Came to Japan.* Berkeley, 1965. An excellently planned anthology of European reports on Japan, 1543–1640, with translations from Latin, Spanish, Portuguese, and Italian sources unavailable to most readers. Comprehensive bibliography.

Kyoto

Dening, Walter. *The Life of Toyotomi Hideyoshi*. Kobe, 1931. Very unscholarly, but the only biography of Hideyoshi in English.

Murdoch, James. *A History of Japan*. Vol. II. *The Century of Early Foreign Intercourse (1542–1651)*. Kobe, 1903. A famous but now somewhat outdated political history.

Sadler, A. L. *The Maker of Modern Japan: The Life of Tokugawa Ieyasu*. London, 1937. Reliable.

Sansom, George. *A History of Japan, 1334–1615*. Stanford, 1961. The best scholarly treatment which includes cultural developments. A detailed bibliography lists mostly Japanese primary sources.

Takekoshi, Yosaburo. *Economic Aspects of the History of the Civilization of Japan*. New York, 1930. Volume I has information on commerce in the Momoyama Period.

Tsuji, Zennosuke. *Nobunaga, Hideyoshi, Ieyasu*. Tokyo, 1943. Popular study by a great scholar. In Japanese.

Religion

Anesaki, Masaharu. *A History of Japanese Religion with Special Reference to the Social and Moral Life of the Nation*. London, 1930. Satisfactory survey.

Boxer, Charles R. *The Christian Century in Japan, 1549–1650*. Berkeley, 1951. Based on a thorough review of all the sources with a very extensive bibliography.

Laures, Johannes. *The Catholic Church in Japan; A Short History*. Revised by Joseph P. Ryan. Tokyo, 1954. Concise.

Suzuki, Daisetz T. *Zen and Japanese Culture*. New York, 1959. Includes chapters about Zen influence on art, *haiku*, and the tea ceremony. Many illustrations.

Tsunoda, Ryusaku, William Theodore de Bary, and Donald Keene. *Sources of the Japanese Tradition.* New York, 1958. Well-chosen excerpts from Japanese philosophers and historians with admirable introductions and a detailed bibliography.

Literature, Theater, and Tea Ceremony

Araki, James T. *The Ballad-Drama of Medieval Japan.* Berkeley, 1964. Well-documented account of the *kowaka.*

Ernst, Earle. *The Kabuki Theatre.* New York, 1956. The best study of the early period in English.

Japanese Classics Translation Committee. *Haikai and Haiku.* Tokyo, 1958.

Keene, Donald. *Japanese Literature: An Introduction for Western Readers.* London, 1953. Brief but excellent chapters on poetry and theater.

Sadler, A. L. *Cha-no-yu: The Japanese Tea Ceremony.* Tokyo, 1930. The standard work covering every aspect of the tea ceremony.

Waley, Arthur. *The No Plays of Japan.* London, 1921. Famous translations with a short introduction.

Art and Architecture

Kirby, John B., Jr. *From Castle to Teahouse, Japanese Architecture of the Momoyama Period.* Tokyo, 1962. Includes all the existing Momoyama buildings in Kyoto. Richly illustrated.

Kitao, Harumichi. *Shoin Architecture in Detailed Illustrations.* Tokyo, 1956. Line drawings and photographs with captions in English.

Kuck, Lorraine E. *The Art of Japanese Gardens.* New York, 1941. Comprehensive appreciation.

Minnich, Helen Benton. *Japanese Costume and the Makers of its Elegant Tradition.* Tokyo, 1963. Careful study with many illustrations in color and a complete bibliography.

Munsterberg, Hugo. *The Ceramic Art of Japan.* Tokyo, 1964. A detailed survey with photographs in color and black and white.

Noma, Seiroku. *The Arts of Japan, Ancient and Medieval.* Tokyo, 1966. Very large, clear photographs with a good text.

Paine, Robert T. and Alexander Soper. *The Art and Architecture of Japan.* Baltimore, 1955. An authoritative general history, well illustrated.

Index

Adams, Will, quoted: 64
Administration of Kyoto: 66
Ainoma: 129
Akechi Mitsuhide: 33ff., 112
Almeida, Luis de, Jesuit missionary: 80
Amaterasu, sun goddess: 88, 90, 107
Ameya, potter: 136
Annalist of Macao, quoted: 55
Aoi matsuri (Hollyhock Festival): 106
Arashiyama: 104
Architecture: *sukiya style*, 120, 123ff., 125; castles, 123–24; *shoin* style, 123–26, 127ff., 142; *shinden* style, 124; *gongen* style, 129
Asagiri Shimanosuke, garden designer: 142
Asahi-hime, sister of Hideyoshi: 39
Asano Nagamasa: 67
Ashigaru: 20, 60
Ashikaga shogunate: 7, 11, 13, 15, 22, 23, 33
August Red Seal: 73
Augustinians: 100ff.
Aware: 112, 116
Awase: 81
Awata: 137
Awataguchi: 73
Azuchi castle: 27, 33ff., 37, 99, 132; described, 124

Bakufu: 7, 11, 13, 21, 55, 95, 144
Basho, poet: 117
Bautista, Pedro, Franciscan missionary: 100–101
Bonsai: 118
Bonseki: 118
Biwa: 114
Biwa, Lake: 8, 33
Buddhism: 12, 21, 27, 32, 35, 88–94, 95, 98, 104, 130, 146
Buke: 11, 16, 58–59
Buke Sho-Hatto: 52
Bugyo: 47, 66
Bushi: 58–59
Bushido: 59
Butai: 111
Byobu: 79

Castles: *see* architecture
Ceramics: Raku ware, 136–38, 140; glazes, 137; Shino ware, 137; Oribe ware, 137; Kyoyaki ware, 137; porcelain, 138
Cha-ire: *see* tea caddy
Cha-jin: 119
Cha'ang-an: 9, 54
Cha-no-yu: 118–22; influence of

Sen no Rikyu, 119; tea house, 119; tea ceremony, 120, 147
Cha-shitsu: 119
Chaya: 74
Chigaidana: 125; meaning of the word, 24
Chikamatsu Monzaemon, dramatist: 115, 147
Children: 64
Chion-in: 33, 91, 106
Chishaku-in: 134
Cho: 10, 55
Chojiro, potter: 136
Chokushimon: 126
Chonin: 58
Chozaburo, musician: 114–15
Cleanliness: 66
Climate: 9
Clothing: 80–85
Cochin: 6
Cocks, Richard, English merchant, quoted: 108
Coelho, Gaspar, Jesuit vice provincial: 99
Concubines: 63
Confucionism: 27, 94–95, 146
Cosme de Torres, Jesuit Superior: 97
Cotton cloth: 72
Craftsmen: 71–74
Crimes: 69
Christianity: 25, 89, 96–103
Chu Hsi: 95

Daibenjo: 79
Daibutsu (Great Buddha): 94, 128, 130, 139; built by Hideyoshi, 39; destroyed by earthquake, 43; rebuilt by Hideyori, 50
Daidairi (Great Palace Enclosure): 9ff., 57
Daigo: 44
Daigo-ji: 141
Daikaku-ji: 133
Daikon: 85
Daimyo: 11, 19–20, 144–46
Daisen-in: 23
Daitoku-ji: 23, 36, 38, 94, 134
Date Masamune: 41
Dengaku: 110
Dengyo Daishi: *see* Saicho
Deshima: 147
Dhyana: *see* Zen
Domin: 58
Dominicans: 100ff.
Donyu, potter: 136
Doshin: 67
Dutch traders: 147

Eastern Hills: *see* Higashiyama
Eaton, William, English merchant: 145
Echigo province: 86
Edo (modern Tokyo): 47ff., 49ff., 55, 60, 71, 73, 101, 109, 133, 144ff., 146, 147, 148
Eisai, monk: 94
Embroidery: 83
Emperor: 4, 15, 56; veneration for, 16; poverty of, 17–18
Enryaku-ji: 8, 90
Eta: 61–62
Executions: 69

Famine: 14
Fans: 84
Fernandez, Juan, Jesuit missionary: 4, 6
Festivals: 106–108
Fires: 11, 21, 68
Food: 85–87; at *Obon* festival, 108
Foreign trade: 74
Franciscans: 100ff.

Index

Frois, Luis, Jesuit missionary: 42, 56, 99; describes Nobunaga, 31–32; quoted, 80, 84; arrives in Kyoto, 97; debates with Nichijo Shonin, 98
Fudai diamyo: 48, 67, 144ff.
Fukuhara: 7
Fujisan: 85
Fujito-no-ishi: 141
Fujiwara: 38, 135
Fujiwara Seika, Buddhist priest: 95
Funerals: 108
Furuta Oribe, tea master: 121, 137, 140
Fushimi: 70, 74, 109ff., 137
Fushimi castle: 27, 41, 43–44, 54, 60ff., 71, 91, 128, 130, 142; built by Hideyoshi, 41ff.; destroyed by earthquake, 43; rooms from, 125–27
Fusuma: 24, 77, 125
Fuyu-no-Jin (Winter Siege): 51

Games: 118
Gardens: 22–23, 120, 141–43
Gates: 126–28
Geisha: 61–62, 114
Gekokujo, meaning of the word: 28
Genji Monogatari: 63, 116
Genkan: 125
Geta: 62, 82
Giboshi: 109
Ginkaku (Silver Pavilion): 13–14, 24, 94, 119
Gion shrine: 14, 89, 106; festival, 107–108
Go: 118
Go Daigo, Emperor: 12
Go Kashiwabara, Emperor: 17
Go Komatsu, Emperor: 24
Go Nara: 6, 17
Go Tsuchi-mikado, Emperor: 17
Go Yozei, Emperor: 40, 95, 109, 115
Gojo (Fifth Avenue): 73; bridge, 21, 57
Gokinai: 8, 16, 30, 66, 86
Gokomachi: 57
Gold Pavilion: *see* Kinkaku
Gongen style: *see* architecture
Gonin-gumi: 68, 95
Gosho, No actor: 110
Goto family: 75, 139
Goto Tokujo, sword designer: 139
Gunki monogatari: 115

Hachiman, Shinto god of war: 89, 107
Haikai: 116–17
Haiku: 117
Hair styles: 81
Hakama: 80ff.
Hakata: 99
Hana matsuri (Flower Festival): 106
Hanami-Yama: 141
Haori: 81
Hara, Katsuro, historian, quoted: 28
Harakiri: *see seppuku*
Hasegawa Tohaku, painter: 134
Hashi: 86
Hashigakari: 111, 113
Hats: 80
Hatsubana: 122
Hayashi Razan, Confucian scholar: 95, 102
Heian-kyo: 9, 25
Heinouchi Yoshimasa, architect: 128
Hidari Jingoro, woodcarver: 126, 130

Hidetada, son of Ieyasu: 48, 49, 51; appointed shogun, 50; persecutes Christians, 102
Hidetsugu, nephew of Hideyoshi: 42, 45, 50, 128; appointed kampaku, 41; commits *seppuku*, 43
Hideyori, second son of Hideyoshi: 43ff., 51, 129; born, 42; meets Ieyasu, 50; defeated at Osaga castle, 52
Hideyoshi: 25, 35, 48, 49, 52, 53, 59, 61, 67, 70, 75, 84, 88ff., 90ff., 100, 103, 107, 123ff., 127ff., 132, 136, 138, 140ff.; one of Three Heroes, 27; governor of Kyoto, 30; changes name, 30; at Nobunaga's funeral, 36; personal characteristics, 36ff.; assumes command, 37; builds Osaka castle, 37; builds Jurakudai, 38; appointed kampaku, 38; erects Daibutsu, 39; his Sword Hunt, 39; entertains Emperor Go Yozei, 40; defeats Hojos, 41; builds Fushimi castle, 41; invades Korea, 42; executes Hidetsugo, 43; receives Ming embassy, 44; visits Daigo, 44; death of, 44; achievements of, 45; bans Christianity, 99; sets out for Odawara, 109; enthusias for No, 110; orders *kowaka* written, 112; verse composed by, 117; holds Kitano Tea Party, 121; rebuilds Sambo-in, 141–42; requires daimyo to live in Kyoto, 144
Hieisan (Wisdom Mountain): 8, 21, 32, 60, 88ff., 90
Higashi Hongan-ji: 92
Higashiyama (Eastern Hills): 8, 10, 13, 25, 33, 137, 148
Higurashi no mon: 127
Hina matsuri (Girls' Doll Festival): 106
Hinin: 58
Hinoki: 76
Hirado: 108
Hitatare: 80
Hiunkaru (Flying Cloud Pavilion): 128
Hizen province: 138
Hojo family: 37, 40
Hojo Ujimasa: 41
Hokke sect: 21, 90ff., 92
Hoko: 107
Hoko-ji: 128
Honami Koetsu, artist: 135, 140
Honda Masanobu: 59
Honen Shonin, priest: 91
Hon-maru: 125
Honno-ji, kowaka play: 112
Honno-ji, monastery: 34
Honshu: 4, 37ff.
Horikawa: 56
Hosokawa family: 13, 15
Hosokawa Fujitake: 56
Hosokawa Katsumoto: 13
Hosokawa Yusai: 117
Hotoke: 108
Houses: construction, 75; roofs, 77; kitchen, 78; living room, 78; privy, 79
Hozu rapids: 105
Hundred Poets' Songs: 17

Ichijo (First Avenue): 10ff., 56
Iemitsu, Shogun: 144–45; expels foreigners, 147
Ieyasu: 33ff., 38, 70, 109ff., 124, 127, 130, 145; one of Three Heroes, 27; marries Asahi-hime, 39; visits Hideyoshi, 39;

rebukes Hideyoshi, 43; family of, 46; personal characteristics, 47; defeats Tairo confederation, 48; chooses Edo as capital, 48; builds Nijo castle, 49; appointed shogun, 49; entertains Hideyori, 50; offended by bell inscription, 51; defeats Hideyori, 52; issues proclamations, 52; death of, 53; collects books, 118; patron of Neo-Confucianism, 95; suppresses Christianity, 102; Nikko shrine of, 146
Iishiro, Tokutomi, historian, cited: 118
Ikebana: 118
Ikko sect: *see* Shin sect
Ireko: 86
Irimoya: *see* roofs
Ima Kumano shrine: 110
Imadegawa: 10
Imagawa Yoshimoto: 29, 46
Inari shrine: 89
Inland Sea: 4, 101, 147
Inro: 139ff.
Ise shrine: 89
Ishida Mitsunari: 47–48, 49, 67, 100ff.
Itakura Katsushige: 67, 102
Ito Ryoton: 38
Izumo shrine: 89, 113

Jesuits: 4ff., 33, 88, 86–100, 101, 102
Jishi-sen: 69–70
Jo: 10
Jodan: 125ff.
Jodo sect: 90–91, 92
Jokei, potter: 136, 140
Joro: 61
Joruri: 113; origins of, 114; theater of, 114
Jurakudai (Palace of Pleasure): 57ff., 91, 109ff., 134, 136, 140; built by Hideyoshi, 38; Go Yozei entertained at, 40; given to Hidetsugu, 41; razed, 43; description of, 127–28

Kabuki: 112, 147; origins of, 113; theater of, 113
Kaeru-mata: 130
Kafuku setsuin: 79
Kagoshima: 4
Kai province: 85
Kaiho Yusho, painter: 134
Kakemono: 131
Kamakura: 7, 11ff., 39, 129, 135
Kameyama, Emperor: 105
Kami: 88
Kami-Kyo (Upper Capital): 57, 88
Kami-shimo: 82
Kammu, Emperor: 7
Kamo River: 8, 10, 24, 57, 72ff., 105, 109, 112ff.; flood, 21
Kamo shrine: 89
Kampaku (Regent): 38, 41ff., 56, 84, 144
Kanami, actor: 110
Kannon: 24, 106
Kano Eitoku, painter: 128, 131, 134; major artist of Kano schools, 132; screens by, 133
Kano Hideyori, painter: 131
Kano Masanobu, painter: 132
Kano Mitsunobu, painter: 132ff.
Kano Motohide, painter: 98, 131
Kano motonobu, painter: 128, 132, 135
Kano Sanraku, painter: 127, 132–33
Kano Tanku, painter: 126ff.; official artist for shogunate, 133

Kanrei (Shogun's deputy): 13, 15
Kanto: 37ff., 40
Kara-e: *see* painting
Kara-hafu: *see* roofs
Karaori: 83
Karasansui garden: 23, 142
Karashishi: 133
Karasuma: 57
Kasuga shrine: 89
Katabira: 81
Katagiri Katsumoto, guardian of Hideyori: 50–51
Katami-gawari: 84
Katana: 80
Kato Kiyomasa: 59
Katsura imperial villa: 121, 146
Katsura River: 8, 35, 105
Kawaramachi: 57
Kawa-ya: 79
Kazari setsuin: 79
Kennin-ji: 128
Kentei, gardener: 142
Kenzan, potter: 147
Kibana: 130
Kii province: 85
Kiku: 141
Kimon: 8
Kimono: 80
Kinkaku (Gold Pavilion): 12, 24, 94, 106
Kinoshita Tokichiro: *see* Hideyoshi
Kiri: 141
Kirishitan: *see* Christianity
Kirizuma: *see* roofs
Kitano shrine: 89, 129; Tea Party at, 121, 128
Kiyomizu-dera (Clear Water Temple): 25ff., 138ff.
Kobe: 7
Kobo Daishi: *see* Kukai
Kobori Enshu, tea master, architect: 121, 143
Kodai-ji: 128ff., 138
Kojiki: 61
Koke-dera (Moss Temple): *see* Saiho-ji
Kokei (Tiger Glen): 142
Kokka Anko controversy: 51
Kokyo: 10
Komparu Hachiro, poet and actor: 110
Konishi Yukinaga: 99
Kora Munehiro, architect: 126
Korea, campaign in: 42, 44, 47, 138
Korin, painter: 147
Koromo: 82
Koshimaki: 82
Koshi-taka shoji: 78
Kosode: 73, 80ff., 83
Kotatsu: 79
Koto: 73
Kowaka: 112
Koyasan: 90, 110
Kuge: 16, 40, 55, 58, 67, 80
Kuge Sho-Hatto: 52
Kujo (Ninth Avenue): 10, 56
Kukai, monk: 89ff.
Kumi-no-oya: 68
Kuno castle: 36
Kura: 78
Kuramaguchi: 56
Kurdo Yoshitaku: 99
Kusemai: 112
Kyogen: 111, 129
Kyogoku: 66, 73
Kyo-Kano: 133
Kyo-yaki ware: *see* ceramics
Kyushu: 4, 37ff., 40, 42, 99, 138
Kwanei era: 55

Lacquer ware: 138–39
Law enforcement: 68–69

Literature: 115–18
Lorenzo, Brother, interpreter: 97–98

Macao: 4
Machigumi: 20
Maeda Geni-i: 56, 66–67, 99ff.
Maeda Toshi-ie, guardian of Hideyori: 47, 110
Magdalen, companion of, Hideyoshi's wife: 99
Maiko: 61
Mairado: 125
Maki-e: 138–39
Makimono: 131
Maria, sister of Yodogimi: 99
Mashida Nagamori: 67, 100
Masks: *see* sculpture
Matsu: 76
Matsubame: 111
Matsudaira, father of Ieyasu: 46
Matsunaga Hisahide: 15, 31, 97, 122
Matsuri: *see* festivals
Meibutsu-kire: 83
Menuki: 139
Meshi: 86
Metal work: sword ornaments, 139; tea kettles, 139; metal fittings, 140
Mikawa province: 46
Mikkyo Buddhism: 90
Militarism: 65–66
Mimi-zuka (Ear Mound): 47
Minamoto family: 12, 33, 49, 141
Minamoto Yoritomo: 11
Minamoto Yoshitsune: 114
Ming Emperor: 43
Mise: 78
Miya: 48
Miyako: 6
Miyabi: 116
Miyoshi: 6, 15
Mizoro: 137
Mizu-ya: 78
Mochi: 28
Momoyama: 41
Money: *Tensho* coins, 75; *Keicho* coins, 75
Mori: 34
Murai Sadakatsu: 66
Murasaki Shikibu, Lady: 63, 116
Muromachi: 14, 38, 73
Muso Kokushi, monk: 22
Myoshin-ji: 94, 133ff.

Nagaoka: 7
Nagasaki: 101
Nageshi: 76–77
Naginata Hoko: 107
Nagoshi Yaemon, metal worker: 139
Nagoshi Yoshichiro, metal worker: 139
Nagoya: 46, 137
Nakamura Masakiyo, architect: 128
Nakasendo: 48
Namban byobu: 85
Namban-ji: (Southern Barbarians' Temple): 98
Nanzen-ji: 94, 134
Nara: 7, 9, 39, 129
Natsuke Masaie: 66
Natsu-no-Jin (Summer Siege): 52
Nature, fondness for: 104–105
"Nembutsu": 91
Nembutsu-odori: 113
Neo-Confuscianism: 95
Netsuke: 138, 140
Nichijo Shonin, monk: 98
Nichiren, monk: 92
Nijiriguchi: 120

Nijo (Second Avenue): 10ff., 73
Nijo castle: 49ff., 51, 58, 60, 97, 124, 134; description of, 127; garden of, 142; visited by Iemitsu, 145
Nijo Palace: 31ff.
Nikko: 53, 130, 146
Ni-no-maru: 127, 142
Ninsei, potter: 147
Nishi Hongan-ji: 62, 92ff., 126–27, 128, 134, 142
Nishijin (Western Camp): 72, 83, 111, 138, 144, 148
Nishinotoin: 73
Niwa: 78
No: 14, 109–12, 113, 129ff.; meaning of the word, 110; description of, 111
Nobunaga: 36, 46, 48, 49, 52, 53, 59, 67, 71, 75, 84, 89ff., 97, 99, 103, 112, 124, 132, 137; one of Three Heroes, 27; family of, 28; personal characteristics, 29; occupies Kyoto, 30; quarrels with Yoshiaki, 30; builds Nijo Palace, 31; described by Frois, 31–32; destroys Hieisan, 32, 90; builds Azuchi, 33; assassinated, 34; achievements, 35; funeral, 36; welcomes Jesuits, 97
Nuihaku: 83ff.

Obi: 81–82
Obon festival: 108
Oda Nobunaga: *see* Nobunaga
Odawara: 37, 40ff., 109
Odoi (Great Rampart): 54, 57, 73
Ogimachi, Emperor: 18, 30
Ohiroma: 127
Oi River: 22
Oji: 9
Okazaki: 46
Okehazama, battle of: 29, 46, 112
Okera bonfire: 106
Okubo Nagayasu: 59
Okubo Tadachika: 102
Okuni, Shinto priestess: 113
Omi province: 86
Omiya: 73
Onin War: 13ff., 18, 20, 54, 56, 107
Ono Harunaga: 51
Organtino (Gnecchi), Jesuit missionary: 33, 98, 100–101
Osaka: 37ff., 48, 51, 54ff., 70ff., 74, 147
Osaka Bay: 4, 7ff., 19
Osaka castle: 27, 40, 43, 50, 99, 102, 124, 126, 132; built by Hideyoshi, 37ff.; siege of, 51–52
Otogi-zoshi: 115
Otowa: 137
Owari province: 28ff., 36, 46

Painting: 130–35; Sung style, 23, 26, 142; Kara-e, 131; Uikyo-e, 131; Yamato-e, 131–32, 134–35; Kano style, 132–33, 135; Tosa Style, 134–35
Philippines: 100, 102
Pillow Book: 116
Pipes: 85
Poetry: 116–18
Politeness: 64
Portuguese clothing: 84
Portuguese merchants: 4, 29, 66, 96, 147

Raku ware: *see* ceramics
Rakuchu: 54
"Rakuchu-Rakugai": 131

Index

Rakugai: 54
Ramma: *see* sculpture
Rashomon: 9, 90
Renga: 117, 147
Reverence for ancestors: 65
Ribadeneira, Marcelo de, Franciscan missionary: 107
Rinzai sect: 94
Rock gardens: 141–42
Rodrigues, João, Jesuit missionary: 100ff.; quoted, 65, 79, 104–105, 114
Roji: 142
Rojin Zatsuwa: 17
Rokujo (Sixth Avenue): 31
Ronin: 20, 34, 51
Roofs: *irimoya*, 125, 127ff; *karahafu*, 126; *kirizuma*, 128; *shichu*, 128; *yatsumune*, 129
Ryoan-ji: 23, 93ff., 106, 141

Sabi: 119
Sacred mirror: 16
Sagoya Sanzaemon: 113
Saicho, monk: 8, 88–89, 90
Saiho-ji: 22, 106
Sakai: 4, 54, 70, 71–72, 74, 97, 121
Sakyo (Left Capital): 9
Sambo-in: 109, 128, 141–42
Samisen: 73, 114
Samurai: 11, 59–60, 116
San Felipe, Manila galleon: 100–101
Sangaku: 59, 110
Sanjo (Third Avenue): 20, 33, 73; bridge, 57, 109
Sanjomachi: 43, 48
Sanjusangen-do (Thirty-three Spaces Hall): 24, 106
Sankin-kotai: 144
Sanno, Shinto god: 90
Sansom, Sir George, historian, quoted: 45
Saris, Captain John, quoted: 86, 101
Sarugaku: 110
Satamura Shokyu: 56
Satori: 92, 94
Satsuma province: 4
Sashimi: 86
Sculpture: *ramma*, 125, 126ff., 130; decline of, 129; masks, 129; *netsuke*, 140
Seami, dramatist: 110, 112
Seikan, priest: 51
Sei Shonagon: 116
Sei-tai-Shogun (Barbarian-subduing Generalissimo): 11
Sekigahara, battle of: 48, 51, 67, 92, 101
Senbondori: 57
Sendai: 41
Sengoku Jidai (Age of the Country at War): 14, 59
Sen no Rikyu, tea master: 119–21, 128, 136ff., 140
Senyo-den: 16
Seppuku: 34, 43, 69
Sesshu, painter: 134
Seto: 137
Shibui: 119
Shichu: *see* roofs
Shijo (Fourth Avenue): 20, 33; bridge, 21, 56, 57, 107
Shikidai: 127
Shikoku: 37ff., 100
Shimabara: 62, 148
Shimo-kyo (Lower Capital): 57
Shin sect: 21, 90ff., 94
Shinden lake garden: 142
Shinden style: *see* architecture
Shingon sect: 89ff., 91ff., 94
Shinmachi: 38

Shino ware: *see* ceramics
Shinran, monk: 91
Shintoism: 65, 88–89, 103, 107
Shirakumo: 122
Shogi: 118
Shoji: 77, 104, 125
Shohekiga: 131, 133, 135
Shoin style: *see* architecture
Shokoku-ji: 134
Shokunin: 72
Shops: 78
Shoshidai (governor of Kyoto): 49, 56ff., 66–68
Shujaku: 9
Shuko, Zen monk: 24, 119
Silver Pavilion: *see* Ginkaku
Samoi, architect, painter: 14, 23
Social classes: 58
Soden, Zen priest: 102
Soin, sculptor: 129
Spainards: 100ff., 147
Streets: 56–57; 73–74
Sugi: 76
Sugoroku: 118
Sui dynasty: 9, 54
Suiboku: 134
Suiko, Empress: 108
Sukiya style: *see* architecture
Sumi: 134ff.
Sumi-e: 117
Sumikura: 74
Sung style: *see* painting
Susanoo, younger brother of Amaterasu: 107

Tabi: 82
Tai-fu: 11
Taiheiki: 116
Taiko (retired regent): 41, 46, 99, 101
Taikoki: 46, 128
Taiko's Sword Hunt: 39, 42
Taira family: 11, 41
Taira-no-Kiyomori: 7
Tairo (regents): 47–48
Takagamine: 135, 140
Takakura: 56
Takamatsu castle: 34, 112
Takao: 105, 131
Takauji, Shogun: 12
Takayama Ukon: 99, 102
Tamba: 67, 73
Tanabata matsuri: 107
Tanegashima: 4
Tanka: 117
Tarashikomi: 135
Tatami: 76, 79, 82, 120; first use of, 24
Tawaraya, weaver: 83
Tawaraya Sotasu, painter: 135
Taxes: 19, 69–70
Tea caddy: 120–22
Tea ceremony: *see cha-no-yu*
Teirin, potter: 136
Teiso, sculptor: 129
Tendai sect: 88ff., 90, 91ff., 94
Tenjo: 77
Tenryu-ji: 22, 84
Teramachi: 57
Textiles: 72, 83–84
Three Heroes: 27ff., 53
T'ien-t'ai: 90
Tobacco: 85
Togu-do: 24
To-ji: 14, 90
Tokaido: 48, 73
Tokonoma: 78, 120, 125; meaning of the word, 24
Tokugawa Hidetada: *see* Hidetada
Tokugawa Iemitsu: *see* Iemitsu
Tokugawa Ieyasu: *see* Ieyasu
Tokusei: 19
Toll barriers: 19
Tosa family: 131, 134–35
Tosa province: 100

Index

Tosa Mitsunobu, painter: 135
Tosa Mitsunori, painter: 135
Tosho Gongen: 53
Toshogu shrine: 146
Toshigoi no matsuri (New Year's Prayer Festival): 106
Toshihito, Prince: 146
Toyotomi Hideyoshi: *see* Hideyoshi
Tozama daimyo: 48, 144ff.
Trousers: *see hakama*
Tsuchi-mikado Palace: 16, 31
Tsuji Yojiro, metal worker: 140
Tsuji-ga-hana: 83
Tsuke shoin: 126
Tsukuno-gami: 121
Tsurumatsu, first son of Hideyoshi: 41

Udaijin: 67
Uji: 86
Uji River: 41
Ukiyo-e: *see* painting
Ukyo (Right Capital): 9ff., 56
Umetada Myoju, metal worker: 139
Unkoku Togan, painter: 134
Uyesugi, daimyo: 47

Valignano, Alessandro, Jesuit visitor general: 65, 99ff.; quoted, 64
Vilela, Gaspar, Jesuit missionary: 60, 80, 97, 107; quoted, 54–55
Vivero y Velasco, Rodrigo de, governor of the Philippines, cited: 105

Wabi: 119
Wakizashi: 80
Women, position in society of: 63

Xavier, Francis, Jesuit missionary: 3ff., 15, 17, 27, 30, 55, 96ff., 99; sets out for Kyoto, 4; letter from, 6; leaves Kyoto, 7

Yaemon, father of Hideyoshi: 36
Yagura: 114
Yama: 107
Yamana family: 13
Yamato-e: *see* painting
Yamazaki, battle of: 35
Yamazaki Sokan, Buddhist priest: 117
Yatsumune: *see* roofs
Yasaka: 37, 107
Yasaka shrine: *see* Gion shrine
Yawata: 43
Yodo River: 4, 5ff., 19, 74
Yodogimi, mistress of Hideyoshi: 41ff., 44, 50, 51–52, 67
Yoriki: 67
Yoshiaki, Shogun: 30, 31, 33, 49
Yoshida Kanetomo: 89
Yoshiharu, Shogun: 15
Yoshimasa, Shogun: 13, 22, 23, 24, 119, 122
Yoshimitsu, Shogun: 12, 16, 22, 24; consolidates power, 12; patron of No, 110
Yoshino: 105, 110
Yoshiteru, Shogun: 6, 15, 30, 97
Yugen: 112
Yuzen dyeing: 72

Za: 19, 20, 68, 71–72; meaning of the word, 18
Za-shu: 18
Zen sect: 22ff., 32, 79, 90, 92–94, 123; influence on No, 111–12; influence on architecture, 124–25; influence on masks, 130
Zori: 62, 82

THE CENTERS OF CIVILIZATION SERIES, of which this volume is the twenty-second, is intended to include accounts of the great cities of the world during particular periods of their flowering, from ancient times to the present. The following list is complete as of the date of this volume:

1. Charles Alexander Robinson, Jr. *Athens in the Age of Pericles.*
2. Arthur J. Arberry. *Shiraz: Persian City of Saints and Poets.*
3. Glanville Downey. *Constantinople in the Age of Justinian.*
4. Rober Le Tourneau. *Fez in the Age of the Marinides.* Translated from the French by Besse Alberta Clement.
5. Henry Thompson Rowell. *Rome in the Augustan Age.*
6. Glanville Downey. *Antioch in the Age of Theodosius the Great.*
7. Richcard M. Kain. *Dublin in the Age of William Butler Yeats and James Joyce.*
8. Glanville Downey. *Gaza in the Early Sixth Century.*
9. Bernard Lewis. *Istanbul and the Civilization of the Ottoman Empire.*
10. Richcard E. Sullivan. *Aix-la-Chapelle in the Age of Charlemagne.*
11. Elizabeth Reifstahl. *Thebes in the Time of Amunhotep III.*
12. Nicola A. Ziadeh. *Damascus Under the Mamalūks.*
13. Edward Wagenknecht. *Chicago.*

14. Arthur Voyce. *Moscow and the Roots of Russian Culture.*
15. Paul Ruggiers. *Florence in the Age of Dante.*
16. Gaston Wiet. *Cairo: City of Art and Commerce.* Translated by Seymour Feiler.
17. Douglas Young. *Edinburgh in the Age of Sir Walter Scott.*
18. Richard Nelson Frye. *Bukhara: The Medieval Achievement.*
19. Walter Muir Whitehill. *Boston in the Age of John Fitzgerald Kennedy.*
20. Arthur J. May. *Vienna in the Age of Franz Josef.*
21. John J. Murray. *Amsterdam in the Age of Rembrandt.*
22. Wendell Cole. *Kyoto in the Momoyama Period.*